THE GUY'S GUIDE
to Surviving TODDLERS, TANTRUMS,
and SEPARATION ANXIETY
(Yours, Not Your Kids!)

Also by Michael R. Crider

From Afar

*The Guy's Guide to Surviving Pregnancy,
Childbirth, and the First Year of Fatherhood*

*The Guy's Guide to Dating, Getting Hitched,
and Surviving the First Year of Marriage*

THE GUY'S GUIDE
to Surviving TODDLERS, TANTRUMS, and SEPARATION ANXIETY
(Yours, Not Your Kids!)

MICHAEL R. CRIDER

Da Capo
∞
LIFE
LONG

A Member of the Perseus Books Group

Designed by Jeff Williams
Set in 11-point Adobe Garamond by the Perseus Books Group

Cataloging-in-Publication data for this book is available from the Library of Congress.

ISBN-13: 978-0-7382-1106-0
ISBN-10: 0-7382-1106-0

Published by Da Capo Press
A Member of the Perseus Books Group
http://www.dacapopress.com

Da Capo Press books are available at special discounts for bulk purchases in the U.S. by corporations, institutions, and other organizations. For more information, please contact the Special Markets Department at the Perseus Books Group, 2300 Chestnut Street, Suite 200, Philadelphia, PA 19103, or call (800) 255-1514, or e-mail special.markets@perseusbooks.com.

10 9 8 7 6 5 4 3 2 1

For Ryan (aka Ry, Ryno, Ryno-flavin, Rybalin, the Ryanator, etc.)—the little boy who has taught me the true meaning of caring, patience and unconditional love. You constantly inspire me and impress me with what a wonderful person you are growing up to be. (Plus you're a funny little fart.) I'm proud of you, little man....

"To be a successful father there is one absolute rule: When you have a kid, don't look at it for the first two years."

—ERNEST HEMINGWAY

CONTENTS

INTRODUCTION

I CAN ADMIT IT; I'm an impatient person. I am a product of twenty-first-century, MTV-fast-cut-edit, short-attention-span, 500-channels-on-the-satellite-and-there's-still-nothing-worth-a-shit-to-watch, Blackberry-carrying, instant-coffee-drinking, cut-to-the-chase-speaking, on-the-go-moving, cliché-hyphen-cliché America. To me, the term *immediate gratification* is a beautiful thing and it pretty well defines my ideal state. In this day and age of fast food, "I Can't Drive 55," high-speed Internet, cell phones, drive-thru coffeehouses, text messaging, thirty-minute photos, outpatient surgery, three-minute pregnancy tests, and digital video recorders that allow me to skip through the annoying commercials on television to get to the crappy twenty-two-minute-long program I've been watching, there is simply no time to wait or waste. And it's not just me—it's me, it's you, and it's every other blue-blooded and Blue-tooth-beaming American out there. We have all become so busy in this new high-tech world that we don't want to wait for information to be given to us.

Here is an example: Have you watched a cable news network in the last few years? Every piece of information you could possibly ask for is on the screen at the same time. I have a forty-seven-inch high-definition television (because, as we all know, life's just not worth living if I can't count the pores on the end of Regis's nose in anything less than 1,400-pixel-per-square-inch resolution). When I watch a news report on one of these channels that simultaneously shows (on various multicolored crawls covering the screen) the time in both EST and PST, the up-to-the-minute sports update, weather update, stock market report, entertainment update, coming attractions of what will soon be coming up on the crawl, and finally (if there's room) some actual news headlines, the anchorperson ends up looking like their head is the size of a postage stamp on my big screen. And yet somehow I can still find a way to be irritated that the one piece of information I was actually looking for is not featured on the screen at that very moment.

I have become so used to instant gratification that some would say it is now officially an addiction. In fact, my wife claims I am addicted to the Internet. This is simply not true. I don't *need* to check my Yahoo e-mail for new messages (mstmrc@yahoo.com). I don't *need* to see if anyone sent me a friend request on MySpace.com. I don't *need* to play poker online and watch as people talk smack via the little chat box down in the corner. I don't *need* to check *Maxim* magazine's "girlfriend of the day" every hour, on the hour. No way. I'm just a recreational user. I can quit anytime I want. In fact, I've gone twenty minutes before without watching that squirrel ride a pair of water skis on YouTube.com. So as you can clearly see, I'm not . . . um . . . OK, fine. It's true! I'm hooked.

I simply cannot stand it if the computer is turned off, if the power goes out, or (God forbid) if my Internet connection goes down. I am a techno-junkie! There is probably a twelve-step program out there for people like me. It'd be like AA, only with initials that are more suitable for Internet users. Something like LOLAA or LMFAOAA. I could walk into a smoke-filled room with folding chairs and a coffee machine, stand up, and say, "Hello. I'm mstmrc@yahoo.com and I am an Internet addict." Then instead of people shouting out, "Hi Mike. We love you," they would express their support by typing instant messages filled with an outpouring of emoticons.

So what, you may be asking, does this have to do with being a parent? (See, you want me to get to the point, don't you? You're impatient, too. I told you so!) It has everything to do with being a parent. The waiting game is the hardest part of early parenting. From the very first moment, we start to question what comes next. When we first thought my wife might possibly be pregnant, I could not stand to wait for the results of the pregnancy test (even the aforementioned three-minute variety). Then when we found out she was pregnant, we couldn't wait to hear the baby's heartbeat each time we went to the doctor's office. Then we couldn't wait to see the baby on the ultrasound screen. Then we couldn't wait to find out the sex of the baby during the aforementioned ultrasound. Then we couldn't wait to meet the baby. And then, after all this waiting for the arrival, I couldn't wait for my son to get through the baby phase.

You see, I was never a big fan of the infancy stage of parenthood. I thought Ryan was cute and instantly loved him, of course. But I didn't really enjoy his company for the first few months. If we're being honest, I think we can all admit this point: for the most part (and how do I put this delicately), babies suck ass. They really do. They don't do anything aside from eat, shit, and bitch constantly. They lie around the house, they keep you up at night, and they don't contribute to anything. I mean, it's not like they add interesting conversation at the dinner table or draw an income. If anything, they drain your income and whittle your dialogue down to nonsensical monosyllabic words. They're worthless. They're like your brother-in-law, only with slightly better social skills. So I couldn't wait until my son would be old enough to hold a conversation. I wanted to be able to laugh with him, share stories with him, watch TV and movies together, play ball, race Matchbox cars with him, and take him to Hooters (for the fine dining experience, of course). I wanted to do anything other than stare at the little bag of flesh that sat on my lap and pooped while I wiped the undigested food and drinks off his face. If I only wanted that kind of company, I'd still be in college. So my impatience, along with my desire to have a little buddy to hang out with, really fueled the fire and made me want to rush the baby process along as quickly as possible.

But then something horrible happened. I got my wish, and my baby boy was no longer such a baby. He was now a little man with thoughts, wants, and a mind of his own. The little baby that could be silenced with something as simple as a pacifier or a brightly colored stuffed animal had turned into a *real live person* with independent thought and the ability to throw a fit at any given time if he didn't get his way. No longer did I have a baby who could be rocked to sleep or would stare at me lovingly with that toothless grin that only babies (or your great-grandmother before she put in her dentures) possess. Now I was faced with a little version of me—funny and well-meaning, but impatient and stubborn. And to make matters worse, he also had inherited my wife's temper. Long story short: I was screwed.

And before I knew it, the baby stage that I had so sorely wanted to pass had done so. And suddenly I was left with the overwhelming desire to hang on tight and not let go of my baby boy. . . .

1

Potty Training—Looking Out for Number Two

FROM TIM, A REAL *GUY'S GUIDE* GUY:

My brother and his wife claimed they would be able to teach their adopted son, Charlie, to use the john before he was a year old, and they would stop at nothing to get this job done. So they listened to a friend of theirs who was a tree-hugging hippie kind of guy. This idiot told them that ten minutes after the baby ate, they should hold his naked body over the sink until he peed or pooped. He also told them to not buy any diapers for the baby, as this would psychologically cause the child to be dependent on them and hinder the process. Being the lemmings they were, my brother and his wife held little Charlie over a sink about twenty times a day to little effect, and wondered why he was having so many accidents in his clothes.

In the meantime, my wife and I had just had a baby a month after my brother and sister-in-law became parents. My brother urged us to try their method of potty training and made cracks constantly about my parenting skills and how I'd be sorry when my son was still in diapers when he was in preschool. All the while my moronic brother and his equally moronic wife were dangling their kid over the kitchen sink, the same sink, I might add, where they were cooking their meals and washing their dishes.

Lo and behold, my son was potty trained by age two, and their son was almost four before he could use the bathroom like a normal kid. But the best part is that to this day my brother won't admit that it was his faulty method of potty training. He told me over dinner not too long ago that he thinks it's because his kid was adopted, and the child had somehow inherited his biological parents' slow learning!

Impatient though I was to have Ryan out of the infancy stage, I have to say that I felt quite torn about the imminent move to the toddler stage and the toddler parenting that would necessarily go with it. Sure, I wanted Ryan to get older, to be more independent and more of a self-sufficient person who didn't need me to wipe his ass every time I turned around. On the other hand, I think it's fair to say that I had my apprehensions about this next phase as well. You see, Ryan was a good baby. He really was. I didn't have a good point of reference—just the public behavior of other peoples' psychotic kids—but I think he was pretty easy to handle. I felt that we had been blessed with a baby who mostly did what he was supposed to do, when he was supposed to do it. Of course he drove me crazy from time to time with the crying and the spittle and the leaving toys all over the room for me to trip on and bust my ass on, not to mention the fact that he sure made it hard for either of his parents to sleep more than three hours at a time. But overall, he was a really good baby. So good that I worried payback would be a bitch. I worried that I was in for a rude awakening once my sweet little angel hit the dreaded terrible twos. I dreaded the moment when my "precious and perfect baby" turned into a "butt-reaming asshole of a toddler." (Before you rip me a proverbial new one for calling toddlers "assholes," you have to keep in mind here that Ryan was our first child so we had no experience with toddlers; heading in we were simply relying on horror stories from more experienced—i.e., worn-out—parents. Give me a break; I was paranoid.) Suffice it to say, I was leery.

Apparently I wasn't the only one in this father/son partnership who was afraid of moving on. It turned out that Ryan was going through some next-phase anxiety of his own. That said, the differences in our anxieties were vast: I was dealing with the emotionally crippling issues spawned from the realization that my only son had evolved from a baby to a toddler, was one step closer to manhood, and no longer needed me to care for him. I was feeling as outdated as a Bill Clinton/Monica Lewinsky joke. I was feeling as useless as a penis in Rosie O'Donnell's bedroom. Ryan, on the other hand, at age two, was dealing with the emotionally (and intestinally) crippling issue of taking a dump on the toilet instead of in his diaper.

And he was not alone. As I understand it, this is a very common phobia among toddlers, especially boys. My son was not ready to give up his diaper days without a fight. He isn't one to surrender his options very easily, and for that I almost admire him. The French could learn a thing or two from this kid. That being said, I knew that he had to submit to potty training. It was time. I didn't want him to be a late bloomer. I mean, after all, I had no real desire to walk him into his seventh-grade homeroom class and say, "Ryan, did you go boom-boom in your diaper-wiper?" So I tried to take charge of the situation and let him know that his time had come. But shit in the can he would not.

What I discovered is that this was a pretty universal problem for parents trying to potty train their children. I'm told that while most children show signs of physical readiness to begin using the toilet as toddlers—between eighteen months and three years of age—not all children have the intellectual or physical readiness to be potty trained at the same time.

What do I mean by "physically" being ready? For the most part you can use common sense to tell when your child might be physically capable of potty training. And yes, I realize that these days, "common sense" is about as "common" as an anorexic white guy winning a heavyweight boxing match. But the fact that you were smart enough to pick up this book means you're pretty intelligent. And good-looking. And successful. (The number-one rule of being an author: kiss your audience's ass.) So since you have that common sense, use it. Obviously, you wouldn't expect a newborn to pee in the toilet (though my wife would argue that a newborn infant might have better aiming technique than I do). But if your child is old enough to know how to use the TV remote (and figure out how to bypass the parental control button to get to the shows they *really* like), then they can probably handle the beginning stages of potty training.

Other signs of physical readiness can include your child's facial expressions (his face turns beet red as if he were Paris Hilton trying to fathom the concept of putting clothes on layaway at Wal-Mart), his body language and posture, what he says (e.g., "I need to drop some fudge off at the ass factory"), staying dry for at least two hours at a time (which is more time than his parents stayed "dry" in their twenties), and having regular bowel movements.

I admit I made some pretty stupid mistakes during my mission to potty train my son. There are things I probably should have done. There are things I might do a little differently today. There are, however, things you should *definitely* avoid while trying to help your child get past the diaper phase. This I know from my own personal experience: You should really avoid beginning the process during a stressful time or period of your family's life (moving to a new house, having a new baby, being named the defendant in a lengthy murder trial, etc.). Choose your timing carefully. Julie and I were looking at selling our house right around the time Ryan began his potty training. This, in retrospect, was a bad idea. We often found ourselves trying to help Ryan feel comfortable with the potty, and our Realtor would call to say that he was coming by with a potential buyer, so we would have to rush our little boy along. This was in no way helpful to our son. Plus, as a home buyer, it's generally a turnoff when you walk into a house that smells like baby shit. *Baking* cookies, yes. *Processed* and *digested* cookies, no.

Here's something else I learned, something you should take to be an irrefutable truth: it's never a good idea to wager with your friends as to when your child will pee in the toilet. And never (and I cannot stress this enough), never double-down on an estimated shit arrival time. This will do more harm than good to your child's potty-training experience (pressure never pays—surely you know this from your own can sitting!), and you'll end up losing one hundred dollars in the process.

Something we never did (and I'm glad we didn't), was to punish our son for having accidents or not making it to the potty in time. I guess we intuitively understood that it certainly is not helpful to the child's mental, emotional, or physical well-being if the parents scrutinize or punish the child for not getting the job done right the first few attempts. I have heard stories of parents scolding their children for not immediately taking to the potty. This is just absurd, and parents like that should be arrested and shot execution-style in the Town Square in front of their peers and colleagues. (OK, that was a little harsh, and maybe I'm unearthing some repressed childhood memories here. *Note to self: call your therapist. . . .*)

The main thing to remember is that this is completely new to the child and it may take them some time to get used to it. After all, they've been using their diaper their entire life and now they're expected to suddenly change their entire way of doing things. It might take them some time. Think about it. Let's say the president interrupted your favorite television show (e.g., *SportsCenter, Star Trek,* a Celine Dion Christmas special from 1997, whatever) and said, "From now on, no one is allowed to pee in the toilet. You must now urinate in an old shoe." It might take you a while to get used to that. So that's why we were able to empathize with Ryan's plight and let him go at his own pace and showed strong encouragement and praise when he was successful. (Incidentally, if you ever have to pee in an old shoe, make sure it's not an open-toed sandal. I'm just sayin'. . . .)

Julie and I did what a lot of new parents do when they aren't sure how to handle the potty-training phase. We asked some veteran parents if there were any tricks of the trade. We heard every method from bribery with candy to shoving laxatives down the child's throat. But the thought of handing our child an eating disorder on a platter like that didn't appeal to us at all. One married couple that we knew (who now I am sure were messing with us to watch us scramble) gave us some interesting advice about potty training. They told us to let Ryan roam around the house naked. This would help him when he realized he had to pee, and he would be able to get to the potty quickly without worrying about pulling down his pants, taking off his training diaper and all that stuff. Well, as I mentioned before, we were trying to sell our house. We didn't want to have stains on the carpet in case he had an accident. Plus this advice sounded just as absurd as the rest of the ramblings of our friends and family.

But then something happened. Or didn't happen, to be more specific. Ryan just wasn't taking to the potty training. He frequently claimed that he needed to go, but his physical actions just never followed through. So I jokingly suggested that we follow the let-him-run-around-all-day advice and see what comes of it. Julie laughed. I laughed. Then we looked at each other like, "Oh shit. We're really going to do this, aren't we?" So, one Saturday when the cable was out and we were bored, we opted to entertain ourselves by letting our little boy run around like he was a hippie at Woodstock (the peaceful one in '69; not the Limp Bizkit let's-tear-a-bunch-of-shit-up-and-set-it-on-fire Woodstock of 1999, which was sponsored by Pepsi and completely lost touch with what the original Woodstock was really about).

Being the paranoid first-timers that we were, we laid towels and bed sheets down on almost every square inch of the floor. Our thought was that if he had an accident, we could simply pick up the towel or sheet, throw it in the washing machine, and the problem would be solved. But somehow, Ryan— being the talented boy that he was (and is)—managed to find the one spot of carpet that wasn't covered and used it as his personal drop box. Sure, we had protected 1,200 square feet of carpeting, but he found a spot that was roughly the size of a credit card to pee on. So when I saw him starting to go, I tried to get him into the bathroom in time to catch some of the golden stream. But when I started toward him, he thought it was a game. He started running down the hallway, naked, giggling and pissing all over the place while his old man chased him around with hands cupped—uselessly, as it turned out—to catch the pee. When I finally got him to the bathroom he had let go of most of his urine and managed to plop a tiny teardrop of liquid into the toilet. And what did his mommy and daddy do? Did we concern ourselves with the pee on our carpet, walls, hands, linoleum, and cat? No. We praised our naked little toddler for the one tiny droplet that made it into the toilet. "Hooray! Ryan went pee-pee in the potty! Good job, buddy!"

After a couple weeks of little to no success with this or any other methods—and after many, many loads of laundry—we turned to the Internet for help. The Internet is a great resource of information, and as I mentioned in the Introduction, I am quite the Internet addict, so I had no qualms about looking for potty training information there. (Of course, if you are one of those people who skipped the Introduction and went right to the first chapter, you probably didn't understand this last reference. Don't blame me. That's what you get for not reading the Introduction. Go back and read it now. The rest of us will wait here until you get back. . . .)

As hard as it is to impress me with facts or findings from the Internet, I have to say that I was amazed at the amount of tools and products sold to help children and their parents cope with potty training. But of course, corporate America knows that this is a big step for families, and not one to be taken lightly. It has therefore capitalized on the fears and desires of unsuspecting parents. The following is an *abbreviated* list of potty training–related products on the market today:

- Potty-training CDs
- Potty-training books
- Potty-training videos and high-def DVDs (the "def" part of high-def in this case probably stands for "defecation")
- Potty-training charts to track your child's success rate
- Potty-training chairs
- Traveling potty chairs (kind of like a porta-potty that sits in your car)
- *Singing* potty-training chairs (nothing disturbing about that . . .)
- Targets for the bottom of the toilet so your child can practice his aim
- Pull-on diapers
- Training pants
- Bed-lining pads
- Sheet protectors (No, no . . . I said *sheet* protectors . . .)
- Bed-wetting pants
- Swimwear made for incontinence

- Musical teddy bears that sing songs about using the potty

- CD-ROM games about toilet training (for the child who has mastered Windows, but still can't figure out where the shit is supposed to flow to)

- Bed-wetting alarms that go off if moisture hits your child's mattress

- Dolls that your child can help potty train, which in turn will help them learn

. . . and there's a good chance that I left out some products. You know what your child really needs for this time in their life? A bagel, a cup of coffee, and the sports section of the paper. That works for most adults (men anyway) on a daily basis, so why couldn't it work for their children? Or maybe all they need to do is walk into a quiet place like a library or bookstore. God knows nothing affects my bowels like walking into a Borders or Barnes and Noble. For whatever reason, a nice quiet area like this causes my stomach to rumble, and I know that it will soon be "go time." Maybe it's all the lattés and scones they sell. Or maybe it's because everyone is being as quiet as a mouse and my stomach likes to play practical jokes on me at these times. Maybe the smell of all that paper reminds me of my home turf and my sports section. I don't know. I don't know why it works. I just know it works. So, in retrospect, maybe I should have taken Ryan into the Sports and Leisure section of my favorite bookstore and his diaper days would have been over a lot sooner.

In our case, Ryan was bound and determined to move at his own pace. Finally, one day when we were outside playing in the yard, he informed me that he had to use the bathroom. So we ran inside, as we had done time and time again, usually with the same result: nothing. But this time was different. Much to my surprise, my little boy used the toilet for what God intended. I was so excited that I practically did cartwheels down the hallway in celebration. I praised him. I hugged him. I told him how proud I was. I hugged him again. I think I may even have clapped at one point, as if what he did was a circus act and I was an excited little kid hopped up on cotton candy. I wanted him to be proud of what he had accomplished in hopes that it would make him want to continue to use the toilet on a regular basis.

But instead of being happy and excited, Ryan started crying. I couldn't believe it or understand why. After all, he had just accomplished a great feat and reached a huge milestone in his life, and that was something he should celebrate. It suddenly dawned on me that maybe he was a little freaked out. Maybe he didn't want to grow up and reach a new plateau in his life. Maybe he was pleased with the way his time on this planet had been spent, and wasn't crazy about changing things. Maybe he was having a hard time accepting the fact that he was no longer a baby. And there it was. All at once I was right there with him. I knew my baby boy was not really such a baby anymore, and as proud as I was, I knew I was going to miss that baby phase. Because let's face it: they don't stay little forever. So as one chapter of my son's life closed and another opened, I knelt down next to my little boy—or should I say "little man"—stroked his hair and asked him if he was going to be OK. And I'll never forget what he said as he looked up at me with those big, tear-filled eyes: "The cold water splashed on my butt and felt yucky."

OK. So maybe he wasn't mature enough to really be "owning" his feelings yet. Maybe he wasn't able to mentally conclude that he was hesitant to take the next step in life. Or maybe his ass was just wet. But either way, it was a very moving experience for us both.

Even after Ryan was fully potty trained, there were still some bizarre rituals that we had to go through in order to get him in the mood to use the bathroom. First of all, he insisted on having one of his parents in the room with him.

And we gladly obliged him, even though this meant having to endure a smelly encounter on a daily basis (hey, we'd gotten used to worse when he was in diapers). Our job description during this time required the following: We had to help Ryan unbutton and remove his pants, sit him on the toilet *just right* so that he could successfully balance himself and not fall in, and we had to face the other direction because he didn't want us staring at him while he pooped. But there was one order that he would bark at us every time, and for the life of me I've never understood why he was so adamant on this point. Every time he sat down to do his business, his first instruction was as follows: "Don't touch my poop." God help me, I still can't figure that one out. But he would tell us that every single time we went into the bathroom with him. As if I were going to reach into the bowl with my bare hands, grab the foul-smelling deposit, and swing it around the room like it was Indiana Jones's trusty whip. "Take that, you Nazi scum! Hiyah!" But I gladly did as I was instructed. Whatever it took to get him to use the bathroom, I was going to do. If he'd asked me to stand on my head and whistle the theme from *Pearl Harbor* as he bombed the crapper, I'd have done it.

Now I don't want you to think I'm pointing out these stories as a way to make fun of my son. That's simply not the case. I'm merely pointing out the ridiculous lengths

Julie and I, as first-time parents, would go to in order to make our kid comfortable enough to move on to the next level. We handled our first (and only) born in a very protective—and yes, probably overly protective—manner, and even though I'm trying harder to relax a bit the older he gets, I'm sure I still do. But this pooping on the potty business was a really huge and important step for us and for Ryan. Though looking back on it, I think it was more of a thrill for us than it was for him and his ass, which, as he pointed out, was now regularly wet from the toilet splash.

Eventually he didn't need me in the room with him while he went, and he got over the paranoia of anyone touching his poop before it was sent through the pipes below the house. And while we were happy that he could now handle the potty-related activities by himself, a part of me realized that this was one less thing in his life that he needed me for. Life was beginning to move too fast. And so were his bowels. . . .

End of Chapter Review Questions

What have we learned here?

1. When beginning to potty train your child, when should you start drinking to avoid strangling the child out of frustration?

a. After he/she cries uncontrollably out of frustration and ends up standing in a puddle of their own piss with a snot-bubble coming out of their nose.

b. When you are chasing after the child (who is running at full speed while taking a shit down a flight of steps) with a wad of toilet paper and screaming, "Come back here, dammit! Daddy is just trying to help you!"

c. A week before you attempt to potty train the child.

2. What is the best store-bought product to help aid the child when he/she is attempting to have a successful bowel movement in the potty?

a. A book on potty training that features cartoon characters using their toilets in a fun, nonintimidating manner.

b. A CD of soft music that helps soothe your toddler and allow her to use the potty successfully.

c. A Shop-Vac to suck the fecal matter right out of her little butt.

d. All of the above.

e. None of the above.

    f. Some of the above.

    g. At the absolute minimum, at least one of the above.

3. Are you regretting your book purchase yet?

    a. No

    b. No

(Do you really think I'd have given you the "yes" option on that one?)

2

....

Because I Said So
(And Other Stupid Things
I've Said to My Son)

....

FROM ZANDER, A REAL *GUY'S GUIDE* GUY:

My wife and I recently caught our daughter Zoe in a lie. She had gotten into the cookie jar and eaten a bunch of chocolate chip cookies before dinner, and then she lied when we asked her about it. She knew better than to get the cookies, because her mom had told her that she couldn't have them a few minutes before. But she did it anyway, and now we had to punish her. Even though it was a pretty harmless lie, it was still enough to get her into trouble. I told her that it was never OK to tell lies. I tried to tell her that telling lies "makes baby Jesus cry," but her mom got pissed at that. She said, "Don't tell your daughter that. Tell her the truth." And so I told my wife that if she didn't like my answers, she should try her hand at it. So my wife, in trying to convince our daughter not to lie, said "if you lie, Santa won't come to bring you any presents." I think we shouldn't have anymore kids.

We've all heard it before. My parents said it. Your parents said it. Their parents said it to them. Hell, even Richie Cunningham's parents said it on *Happy Days*: "Because I said so."

Whenever you wanted to do something as simple as buy a chocolaty treat from the grocery store, go spend the night at a friend's house, go to a movie, or even do something as harmless as, say, jump naked from atop the city's water tower, it seemed like your parents always said no. And when you inevitably asked why, their answer was always the same: "Because I said so."

Those four words were indisputable. "Because I said so." The words themselves, when placed together side-by-side, simply couldn't be beaten. Once your parents said that little phrase, game over. Nothing you could say could possibly one-up it. It was a done deal. Fin (for you fans of artsy-fartsy foreign independent films).

My parents were the king and queen of "Because I said so." When I was about fifteen (and might reasonably have been beyond the power of "Because I said so," but wasn't— hey this isn't about my maturity level. Can't you tell that I've moved slowly in that department my whole life?), I wanted to get my ear pierced. I wanted to be rebellious (albeit in an incredibly conformist way, as everyone else I knew and hung around with was doing it). But I thought I had a better chance of having my way if I respectfully went to my parents and asked for their blessing on putting a hole in my body. My logic was that if I didn't go off and pierce my ear behind their backs, it would show them that I had the maturity to handle the responsibility like an adult. I'm not sure what kind of responsibility went along with having one's ear pierced, but look at this from my perspective: assuming that adult responsibility was something they wanted me to have (see the pattern here—everyone wants their kid to grow up already!) and I was trying to show them that I was up to the task (admittedly, by trying to beat them at their own game). Really, how could they say no to such an honest and decent kid?

Well, they said it kinda like this:

"No."

I was stunned and needed to come up with an argument quickly. I asked them why and what their problem was with the thought of their only son punching a gaping hole in the side of his head for no good reason. They had a list of reasons that included, "It'll get infected," "You'll look like a girl," and "What will the people in church think?" I countered their oppositions with "I'll clean it every night with alcohol," "Nu-uh," and "I'll take it out when we're at church." Knowing that I had now convinced them to change their minds, I waited for their reply, which now had gone from "No" to . . . "*We said no!*" At this point, I probably stamped my foot, held my hands up in amazement and once again asked them why not. Tired of hearing me argue, they laid down the granddaddy of all comebacks:

"Because we said so."

And that was the end of the argument. What more could I say? Sure, I could have done it anyway and suffered the consequences—being grounded and having the earring ripped from my still-sensitive flesh. Or I could have run away from home and lived my life exactly the way I wanted. Go figure—I didn't see these as viable options. (It wasn't until a year or two later that I finally convinced them to let me pierce my ear, and I've now had both of them pierced for nearly two decades . . . and without a single infection, might I add. Ha! I win. . . .)

But at that point I vowed that I would never, ever treat my kids the way my parents treated me. I would treat them with the respect they deserved, I wouldn't treat them like they were young or stupid, and I certainly wouldn't use the same old "because I said so" answers that they used against me. I was going to be an evolved parent, and nothing would change my mind or stand in my way. But then something happened:

I had a kid.

Starting around the time Ryan became a toddler, I used the word *no* more times in my everyday life than I used words like *it, then,* or even *antidisestablishmentarianism,* a word I use almost hourly. (OK, so I don't use that word at all. But it's such a cool word—and the longest in the English language—that I wanted to try and work it in here, just to make myself sound smart.) He would ask me for a cookie—his fifth sweet treat in the same amount of time it takes for a commercial about the cookie he now desires to air—and I would say no. He would ask for a toy at the store every single time we'd walk through the door, and nine times out of ten I'd say no. He'd ask for a puppy, and I'd say hell no. He'd ask for a younger brother or sister and I'd . . .

well, I'd black out and wake up a couple of hours later. But then when I recovered from the smacked-my-head-on-the-linoleum trauma, I'd tell him no. He'd try to plug the cat's tail into the VCR and I'd have to scream "No!" from across the room. He'd take his crayons and "redecorate" the wall in the hallway, and I'd have to once again say no. By this point in the day it was usually blessedly time for bed, a fact about which I would inform him. And then he would tell *me* no. But for the most part, I was the one giving him the big N word.

At first, Ryan would just accept the order barked at him and go on about his little life. But eventually, as is a tradition passed down for hundreds of generations, my son learned to question what he was starting to consider unfair treatment. His inquiry was the inevitable and ubiquitous "Why?" And when I couldn't think of any other reason other than I just wanted him to shut up—as is a tradition passed down for hundreds of generations—I actually said, "Because I said so." And then I—as is also a tradition passed down for hundreds of generations—discovered that this answer seemed to pacify his curiosity and desire, and I suddenly knew why my parents used it on me. It was the perfect answer!

At this writing, I've been a parent for seven years and along the way I'm happy to report that I've added a good number of words and phrases to my arsenal of effective things to say in my day-to-day parenting. Some of these phrases are filled with wisdom: "Don't set fire to the cat's tail or she'll probably die."

Some of them are just enough to pacify my son: "That's right, Ryan. Thunder isn't anything to be afraid of. It's just God bowling with Jesus."

And others (if I may be so bold as to admit this) are just flat-out stupid. These include, but aren't limited to, the following sentences:

"If you throw up, I'm going to spank you."
"Oh, don't act like a little four-year-old."
"Mommy's penis fell off because she told a lie."
And, of course, that old standby: "Because I said so."

Allow me to explain. Let's start out with what was quite possibly the dumbest thing I've ever said, particularly if taken out of context:

"If you throw up, I'm going to spank you."

Now, this is the mother of all stupid things to say to a child. And I understand that, to an outsider, this comment seems harsh and cruel, almost to the point of abusive. But please don't call the authorities on me just yet, because this was an empty threat at best. Just allow me to explain.

Before my son was six years old, getting him to take cough and cold medicine was a huge ordeal. If he were faced with the unthinkable task of putting what amounts to purple Kool-Aid with an antihistamine in his mouth, he would fight us every step of the way. Ryan—usually an exceptional child when it comes to being well-behaved (again, based on my vast body of knowledge in these areas)—would cry, kick, scream, flail around, and act as if we were torturing him. We would sit him down on the couch, give him the tiny shot glass–sized medicine cup and tell him that if he just took his medicine he'd feel better. But you'd have thought we were asking him to ingest liquid cyanide, the way he rebelled against this.

First came the sealed-lip cry. This was what we called it when he clamped his mouth shut as if it were lined with Super Glue. Additionally, tears and fear-induced snot would flow down his face and he'd start a muffled yet agonizingly sad wail. We'd ask him to open his mouth and all we'd get in return was "Mmmmmmmmmphhhhhmmmmmphhh," which I think may have been him telling us in toddler terms to go fuck ourselves. Then we'd try bribery by telling him that we'd give him a cookie, piece of candy, whatever it took to get him to calm down and take his medicine like a man. There were times when I'd gladly have offered to buy him a new car if he'd just get this ordeal over with. Hey, maybe I should have tried that.

Sometimes the promise of sweets would get him to at least break the seal and we'd briefly think that we had won the battle once and for all. But we would soon find that our victory was short lived.

Ryan would then take the cup from our hand, hold it up to his mouth, and then announce that he had to go pee. I would tell him that he could pee after he took the half friggin' teaspoonful of medicine, and his mommy would inevitably undercut my authority and say, "No, it's OK. Go pee, then come back and take your medicine." At this point my wife and I would exchange angry glances and Ryan would take this time to escape into the bathroom for a very prolonged potty experience. I've got to hand it to him: this was a nice stall tactic, even if it was blatantly obvious. Really, the kid could stall in there: If I didn't know better, I'd have sworn he had the prostate of a seventy-year-old man. Once he finally reappeared he would hold the cup, take a deep breath, and move it toward his mouth. At this point, Julie and I would be holding our breath in anticipation, hoping against hope that this would soon be over and done with. He would then tilt the cup, take an atom-sized sip of the medicine, and immediately start crying again.

"It's icky," he would tell us as he squealed through his tears. Then as we were trying to convince him to drink it quickly, his hair-trigger of a gag reflex would kick in. Usually he would only gag and cry, but every now and then he would manage to conjure up real live vomit (just to spice things up a bit, I imagine).

The pattern never seemed to change. Every time he had a cold, I dreaded these moments, as these antics became more and more tiresome. Finally one time, frustrated after twenty minutes (no kidding, twenty minutes) of trying to talk my son into taking his cold medicine, I snapped. He went through the usual routine of clamping his mouth, peeing, and finally gagging. Feeling my blood pressure skyrocket, I actually said to my toddler, "If you throw up, I'm going to spank you."

I really don't know what I was thinking, other than the fact that nothing else seemed to work and I had reached my limit. Julie looked at me as if I had lost my mind, and just as I was getting ready to tell her and her son where they could go for the rest of eternity, we both busted out laughing. We both realized how ridiculous this entire thing was, and were giddy with exhaustion. Ryan even laughed, and relaxed just long enough to take his medicine without vomiting. So I finally realized what would make my son do as he's told: driving his parents to the brink of insanity. (Gee, I can't wait until he proves this theory as a teenager as well!)

"Oh, don't act like a little four-year-old."

In this instance, my point was for him to act his age and stop being so immature. But in my haste, I forgot one little thing. Ryan was only three at the time. So I guess if he were acting like a four-year-old, he'd have been acting mature beyond his years. I'm such an idiot. . . .

"Mommy's penis fell off because she told a lie."

I know what you're thinking: what in the world kind of question could have prompted this explanation? Honestly, I was just being funny—this was just a joke, but sometimes I forget that children don't always understand sarcasm. See, when my son was two years old, he accidentally walked in on Julie getting out of the shower and as a result saw his mommy in her birthday suit. He was in a rush to tell her something and so he busted in the bathroom, stared at his mother's nude body, and, with mouth and eyes wide open, screamed out: "Mommy! Where'd your penis go?" This was one of my all-time favorite Ryan moments, and I laughed until I thought I was going to die.

Once I regained my composure, I asked my wife how we should deal with his question. Should we be honest with him? How much should we tell him? Will this cramp I got in my side from laughing ever go away?

She and I both felt that we should be honest with him and explain that boys have penises and girls have vaginas, but we agreed he was still too young to need to know or understand how the plumbing matches up and why. We then argued for the next twenty minutes over who should be the one to tell him this. After I lost the coin flip, I got to sit our two-year-old down and unveil life's secrets.

So, in a panic with nothing else to say, I told Ryan that his mommy's penis fell off because she told a lie. At this point, Julie threw me out of the room and told our little boy the truth about the male and female anatomy. Some people just don't appreciate good sarcasm when they hear it.

"Because I said so."

I don't need to explain this one any further. Why? Because I said so.

End of Chapter Review Questions

What have we learned here?

1. What are the four most essential words to remember in parenting a moody, headstrong toddler?
   a. Stop, drop, and roll.
   b. Because I said so.
   c. I scheduled a vasectomy.
   d. All of the above (*Hey!* That's a four-word phrase also! Cool!).

2. What were Richie Cunningham's parents' names on *Happy Days*? Seriously. I can't remember. Can you?

3. Did you really just count on your fingers to see if "all of the above" was actually a four-word phrase?

3

I'm Turning Ryanese,
I Think I'm Turning Ryanese,
I Really Think So

FROM DOUG, A REAL *GUY'S GUIDE* GUY:

My wife is a youth minister and the associate pastor of our church. Our son, Jack, had a speech impediment that made it hard for him to say his "T's" or his "R's" very well, or at least the "T's" and "R's" at the beginning of his words. If these letters were at the end of the word, it never seemed to be a problem. It was just that darn beginning "T" and "R" that would give him fits. Jack was playing in the church nursery when he was about two years old. His favorite toys were Hot Wheels and other small cars like that. He had been playing with his cars when one of the other children took the toys away from him. Suddenly, my wife gets a call in her office: the day-care provider asked her to come down the hall to the church nursery. When she got there, the day-care worker told her that Jack had been saying bad things. My wife asked what was said, but the young lady was too embarrassed to repeat what Jack had said. Finally the worker said with a red face, "Jack told the other kids to give him the f—ing cars." My wife was humiliated, as you can well imagine. So she grabbed our son by the arm and asked him if he knew what he was saying. Once he explained it to her, she finally realized that Jack was trying to say, "Give me the TRUCK 'n' cars." My wife told the day-care worker the truth, and speech therapy soon followed for my boy.

From the moment Ryan uttered his first word (which was "Mama," much to his daddy's dismay) two things have been a constant in the Crider household: Ryan's never stopped talking, even in his sleep. (He babbles on like an auctioneer, speaking as fast and furiously as he can, and talks about every subject known to man, often without segue.) And ever since he began speaking, I've been trying to figure out what the hell he was talking about.

At first, his little brain was working faster than his mouth could keep up. And as a result he would come up with these little nonwords or phrases that his mother and I would have to try to decode.

"Stop"—if he saw a stop sign and wanted to acknowledge it (or tell his mother that in her erratic driving, she forgot to stop at the big red sign)—inexplicably became "po."

"Ryna" was his way of saying "Ryan."

"Brefakst" was his way of saying that he was hungry in the morning.

Hardly anything came out the way it was supposed to, as is the case with all toddlers when they first begin speaking. (Right? Or has everyone just been trying to make Julie and me feel better?)

I loved this stage, because I really dug how Ryan was trying to coordinate what he was trying to say with the way he was actually saying it. And trying to decipher his words became a fun game for us. It was like playing a live game of "Word Jumble." But with all of the things he couldn't say correctly, he had one true talent, and that was the ability to enunciate swear words as clear as any mature person or comedian on the Def Jam Comedy show.

When you first have a baby, someone at a baby shower will undoubtedly provide you with a book in which you can jot down the baby's "firsts." These books usually have a heading at the top of each page that says something like, "Baby's First Step," "Baby's First Tooth," "Baby's First Word," "Baby's First Date," "Baby's First Senior Prom," "Baby's First Wedding," "Baby's First Baby," "Baby's First Divorce," "Baby's First Retirement Party," "Baby's First Eightieth Birthday Party Where He's Comatose and Doesn't Know He's Even There," "Baby's First Coffin," and other various firsts. And below each heading is a big blank area so that you, the proud parent, can fill in the date and detail of each first. What they don't provide (and now that I'm a parent, I truly think they should) is "Baby's First Cussing Fit."

I have to admit that I possess the sense of humor of a twelve-year-old at a slumber party (snickering while watching *Real Sex* on HBO without their parents knowing about it). Even though I do relish highbrow jokes that really make you think, there is another part of me that truly just loves a good dirty joke. Let's face it, I've penned what amounts to a collection of dick and fart jokes for the majority of my writing career. So it should come as no surprise that a good cussing fit will throw me into hysterics, and I'll laugh like a stoned frat boy watching a *South Park* marathon. As funny as I think "bad words" are on a normal basis, nothing is funnier to me than when either a really elderly person swears or when a small child swears.

I'll never forget my son's first swearing experience. Julie and I were on the couch watching television and little three-year-old Ryan was playing on the floor in front of me. Being heavily into Thomas the Tank Engine, Ryan had an enormous and ridiculously expensive wooden train track set up in the middle of the room. Using the imagination that only a toddler has, he had built an entire city around a large number of talking trains. These engines would tell each other stories, hold conversations about their daily lives, and sing songs, all utilizing the same narrator, my son. At one point during the play period, Ryan had attached all of the trains together and they were zooming around the wooden track at breakneck speed with Ryan as their accelerant. As was the usual routine, he was on his knees, crawling around the room with one hand on the front engine (Thomas). Usually, they would go round and round the track until Ryan got dizzy or tired. But this particular time, something different happened.

As Ryan was making his way around the circular track, his trains collapsed on their side. He'd gone too fast and the trains lost their grip on the track. Normally he would have just stood them up, reset them and gone about his business. Instead, he slammed his fist down onto the carpet and yelled, "Well, shit!" My wife and I looked at each other, our mouths both wide open in disbelief at what we had just heard. We both knew right away that we needed to correct him and make sure he didn't utter that word again. We both also knew that *she* was going to have to be the one to tell him this, because I was turning red-faced from trying to hold in my laughter.

Plus the irony was not lost on me that the person who probably taught him that word in the first place would now have to be the one to teach him that it was wrong for him to say. We both knew that he got the word *shit* from his mommy. Later when he would yell out the word *goddammit*, we would both know that his daddy was responsible for that one. But this time around, it was all Julie's doing. So it was up to her to fix the situation. I'd have volunteered to help, but I was too busy laughing my head off.

So Julie took her baby boy into the next room and explained to him that there were good words and there were bad words. He seemed to grasp this concept very quickly. And I say this with confidence because from that moment on, he admonished me constantly whenever I used any "bad words." And let me tell you that you just haven't lived until you've been punished by a toddler for using the word *shitty* to describe your day.

As time went on, Ryan's vocabulary grew almost as quickly as he grew out of his shoes. And just as quickly, I had gotten bummed out over something I'd been looking forward to for months, even years. I discovered that as much as I liked hearing him speak in a grown-up manner and using more adult phrases, I missed the baby words he used. Before I could talk to him in his own "Ryanese" and all was well with the world. Now suddenly when I asked him what he wanted for "brefakst," he looked at me like I belonged on the short bus. He had somehow grown out of that sweet little baby-talking stage right before my eyes, and as proud as I was of him, I was starting to see the writing on the wall. He was one step closer to being a little man. Soon he'd be saying, "Oh Father? I beg your pardon, and do hate to be a bother. However I was wondering if I might trouble you to briefly pontificate upon the latest NATO trade agreement and how it will have an adverse effect on third-world countries. . . . " Or he'd outsmart me with his own pontification on the subject. Or he'd not engage me in the conversation at all—instead choosing his peers for conversation.

And I realized that I wasn't remotely ready for this.

End of Chapter Review Questions

What have we learned here?

1. When teaching your child to speak correctly, which of the following tools is *not* appropriate?
    a. A Speak & Spell toy.
    b. Educational television programs like those found on PBS, Nickelodeon, or C-SPAN.
    c. Flash cards that utilize simple key words and phrases.
    d. Richard Pryor's *That Nigger's Crazy* album.

2. What are some key phrases you need to teach your child when they first learn to speak?
    a. I love you.
    b. I'm hungry.
    c. I need to go pee-pee.
    d. Michael Jackson is at the front door. Dial 911.
    e. All of the above.

4

Why? Or, A Conversation With a Toddler

FROM TODD, A REAL *GUY'S GUIDE* GUY:

My wife and I were in a Wal-Mart with our eighteen-month-old son Reagan just before Christmas. He had just started this thing where he threw a fit every time he didn't get a new toy when we went into the store. My wife blamed this on me because most of the time if I took Reagan anywhere, we got a toy or a treat. I thought I was being nice, and I wanted to get something for my son since I don't get to go out with him alone very often. Anyway, we were in the store doing some Christmas shopping for our friends when

Reagan saw a new toy car that he wanted. It was one of those cars that light up and blare really loud music when you push a button, and he decided that he wanted to have it. I told him no, and he started to cry. "Why?" he kept asking me over and over. I told him that it was too close to Christmas and that Santa would be bringing him lots of toys, maybe even that toy car. His crying got louder and he started screaming "Why me, God? Why me?" (Did I mention that he has a real knack for being dramatic?) We tried to calm him down and offer a compromise by giving him a piece of candy if he would just stop crying. But as we soon learned, reasoning with a toddler is next to impossible. The conversation was going nowhere and he wasn't calming down. He just kept asking God why he couldn't get a toy. So instead of doing our Christmas shopping that day as a family, we left empty-handed. Well, I guess I wasn't empty-handed. I was carrying a kicking and screaming child.

There are clearly elements to being a dad to a newborn that are difficult and frustrating. That's a given, and I knew that going in. One of the worst things to deal with was not knowing what was wrong with my little guy when he was upset. My son would cry, I would have no idea why, and this would send me into a panic. Babies cry for what seems like an eternity for what appears to you to be no real reason. Of course in reality we know they have their reason. They're either tired, hungry, gassy, or just like hearing the sound of their own voice at full volume from time to time. This can be increasingly frustrating if you don't know what they want, and you find yourself wishing they could tell you exactly what they want. And at these times, I remember I would think to myself how wonderful life would be once Ryan was old enough to walk up to me and, using words, let me know exactly what he wanted or needed. Until then, I would just have to do some troubleshooting until I discovered exactly what the problem was. I'd stick a bottle in his mouth, and he'd keep crying. I'd check to see if his diaper had been soiled, but he kept screaming. Eventually we'd resolve it, of course. I might change his clothes, and he'd stop crying—perhaps the tag in his onesie had bothered him or maybe he really wanted to wear green instead of white. Or I might go find Julie, and he'd stop crying—is it possible that he had been as tired of looking at me as I had been of looking at him? Who knows? As I'd hoped, once he became a walking, talking toddler, Ryan was able to tell me what was wrong or let me know whatever it was he desired. There's certainly some satisfaction in that—no more guessing what's got him bothered.

But he was also able to start asking questions. He had one particular question that he liked to ask on a constant basis, and as it turns out, it's by far the most-often-asked question among toddlers. And it's the one question that, in theory, should be relatively easy to answer. It's a question that is simplistic in its core meaning, but is always followed up with more questions. And that question is . . . "Why?"

At first, I appreciated Ryan's inquisitive nature. I realized that by asking why something happened or why something was the way it was, he was building life skills and was on his way to becoming an intelligent little person. But after a while, hearing the very word *why* (or even words with the letter "y" in them) grated on my nerves so badly that I would much rather have taken an ice pick up the urethra than ever hear that question again. You may think I'm being insensitive or impatient by not wanting to answer a few questions. But these weren't a few questions. The attorneys in the O. J. Simpson trial asked a few questions. A senatorial committee that meets to discuss whether or not to impeach a president for sticking a Cuban cigar into a female intern's mommy parts has fewer questions than a toddler. (Again, I know that is an outdated reference, but dammit if it isn't still funny as hell.) And if your child is beginning this dreaded "why" stage, rest assured that you'll soon be fielding an unbelievable amount of questions, too. And I would venture to bet that you'll be like me, wishing you could have held onto the baby phase a little bit longer. Babies make a lot of noise, but you don't really always have to pay close attention to their ramblings! Not so with a toddler.

This is a typical conversation between Daddy (that'd be me) and my toddler (played by Ryan):

DADDY: Ryan, don't run with that stick, little buddy.

RYAN: Why, Daddy?

DADDY: Because you might fall down and hurt yourself.

RYAN: Why?

DADDY: If you fall down on the stick, you might puncture yourself and I'd have to take you to the doctor.

RYAN: Why?

DADDY: If you puncture yourself, you'll have to have stitches.

RYAN: Why?

DADDY: So you'll heal properly.

RYAN: Why?

DADDY: So the wound doesn't become infected and possibly become a festering, gangrenous, pus-seeping hole that your mother might notice during your bath time and get pissed at me for.

RYAN: Why?

DADDY: Because Mommy tends to nag Daddy once in a while.

RYAN: Why?

DADDY: I'm just kidding. She doesn't nag me. She knows that we both have the same goal, which is to make sure you're happy and safe.

RYAN: Why?

DADDY: Because she and I want to take good care of you.

RYAN: Why?

DADDY: Because we love you.

RYAN: Why?

DADDY: Right now, I'm not really sure why. Frankly, you're starting to irritate the ever-loving shit out of me.

RYAN: Why?

DADDY: Because you're asking too many questions.

RYAN: Why?

DADDY: Because you're apparently very inquisitive.

RYAN: Why?

DADDY: (sigh) I don't know. Maybe you think you're Carl Sagan or something and need to know the meaning of life right this instant, when all I'm trying to do is to *get you to stop running with the damn stick!*

RYAN: Why?

DADDY: You know what? I don't even care anymore. Run with the stick. Run like the wind.

RYAN: Daddy?

DADDY: Yes, Ryan?

RYAN: I love you.

DADDY: Awww . . . I love you, too.

RYAN: Why?

End of Chapter Review Questions

What have we learned here?

1. Why?

5

··

Mr. Mom

··

FROM STEVE, A REAL *GUY'S GUIDE* GUY:

When I first told my dad that I was going to be a stay-at-home father, he said he thought I was crazy. He is really from the old school and said it was "woman's work" to take care of the babies. I just let it go in one ear and out the other because I knew he wouldn't approve no matter what I did. So once my wife had our twins, I became "Mr. Mom." After a couple of months of changing diapers, dealing with sleep problems and all that, I wanted to give up. I was so frustrated with everything that I just wanted to go back to work and let my wife do all the parenting. I was telling my dad this on the phone one day while I was having a nervous breakdown. I knew he'd be on my side because, as I said, he was from the school of thought that believes mothers should stay home with the children. Instead, he jumped my ass and said, "What's wrong, little girl? Did your dress get stained while playing house?" He told me to buck up and get over my problems, because it was my duty as a dad to take care of the twins no matter what and I didn't get to complain, because this is what I chose. So I guess by his logic, I was being a woman if I stayed home with the kids and being a woman if I bitched about staying home with the kids and wanted to quit. I can't win.

I toughed it out and now the twins are in elementary school. I look back on those days as hard, but I also see them as good memories. The house is empty for a few hours and I kinda miss the kids. We're thinking about having more kids, and I think I'd be Mr. Mom all over again. I liked playing that role. I wouldn't admit that to my dad for fear of being labeled a girl again, but I can say it here because I seriously doubt that he'll read this book. If it's not a war novel or the Auto Sales section of the paper, he doesn't read it.

Julie and I decided early on (even before Ryan was born) that I would be the one to stay home with him. We reached our decision by agreeing on the following:

We wanted at least one parent at home with Ryan at all times.

We didn't want our child going to a day-care facility.

Julie had a better and higher-paying job (mainly because she didn't drink herself out of college like I did and so she managed to get herself a real job) so it made sense for her to work and for me to be the one to stay at home.

Now let me say this right off the bat so I don't get angry letters from parents with children in day care, or people who own or work in a day care, or from anyone who was in a day care and felt the experience did them a great service: I understand the need for day care. I know that a large number of families in this country and around the world have to have dual incomes, which means they have to have their children cared for outside of the home. I don't think you're a bad parent for putting your child in day care. I understand your plight and see where you're coming from. You're doing the best you can, and to repeat: you're not a bad parent. I just happen to think that I'm better than you. (Just kidding. No need to fire up your e-mail account and call me bad names IN ALL CAPS just yet. . . .)

I stayed home with Ryan from the time he was born until he was four years old. I dealt with everything. I saw the good, the bad, and the ugly. I shoved the food in the top end and wiped it when it came out the back end. I saw the first step, and bandaged up the first boo-boo. I heard the first word, and took the brunt of his first rant. I didn't miss a single "first" moment of his early years, and for that I'm grateful. But I do understand that being a stay-at-home father isn't for everybody. It's a tough gig to pull off, and sometimes it's even tougher for people to accept.

When Julie and I decided that I would be the one parent to stay home, our decision was met with varying opinions. Some thought it was fine, but others—usually those from earlier generations—didn't much care for the idea. It amazed me that somehow the fact that I wanted to care for my child in a somewhat unorthodox, yet entirely natural, manner would be met with negative reactions. I got earfuls about how it is the "woman's job is to stay home with the baby" and how I should be the breadwinner of the family. With the occasional sneer, I was called Mr. Mom and was made to feel sort of emasculated or like someone who was "bumming off of his wife" simply because I was caring for my child, which was something that felt normal to me. But once it all came down to it, we decided that what we were doing was right for our family, and damn anyone else who would think differently.

I think that maybe I should explain the term Mr. Mom here, and why I really don't enjoy that moniker. Mr. Mom is a term coined in the early '80s and based on a movie by the same name. It starred Michael Keaton as a hapless father who loses his job at an auto manufacturer and is then thrust into the role of taking care of his children when his wife goes back to work. The comedic premise revolved around the notion that men are too inept and stupid to take care of their own children. So you had the children walking around filthy, the kitchen was on fire, the washing machine was overflowing because he, being a man, was too stupid to know how to do laundry. The movie really was insulting, if you think about it. After all, if there was a comedic movie in this day and age about a woman working in an accountant's office and was completely lost because of the old stereotype that "math is too hard for women," NOW would have your ass on a platter, and women would be protesting from coast to coast (during their lunch breaks from Big Accounting Firms). They'd all be holding up picket signs that said things like, "2,4,6,8 . . . this movie is one we really hate!" and shit like that. But make fun of a man who wants to raise his children, and suddenly it's acceptable. After seeing this movie, I always felt the term Mr. Mom was derogatory and translated into "moron who is delusional and thinks he has a chance in hell of raising children without burning down the house in the process." I've been called Mr. Mom ever since I first started staying home with my baby boy, and I've done my best to dispel the myth that fathers cannot hold their own in the world of parenting. And it seems that I wasn't alone.

It turned out that I was sort of in the beginning of a climate shift in parenting, as a lot of fathers were choosing the stay-at-home route. In previous decades, it was highly abnormal for the man of the house to stay at home and raise his children. In the 1950s, only tens of thousands of fathers took an active role in parenting. Most others were at the office all day and would expect their children to be in bed once they were home, and wanted their wallflower wives (donning a freshly pressed skirt and apron) to have the perfectly prepared four-course dinner hot and ready the second they walked in the door. After which, she would faithfully service her caveman-esque husband and expect nothing in return. As time marched on and women became more prominent in the workforce, the tables began to turn on the old *Ozzie-and-Harriet* style of American life. In fact, by the time I had entered my second year of being a stay-at-home dad in 2002, the number of fathers in the United States doing what I had been doing for two years had reached upwards of three million. Now of course, that's only about 1 percent of the U.S. population, but it was a significant increase from past decades. Fathers were taking a more hands-on approach to parenting. Ozzie was rolling over in his grave, and Harriet was burning her bra while screwing the intern in the mailroom at the major corporation where she was the CFO. The times they were a changin'. . . .

Buoyed by the knowledge that there might be other dads out there doing the same thing I was, I went looking for some fellow Mr. Moms with whom to share this experience. I looked in the local newspaper and found an ad for a group of SAHDs (which stands for stay-at-home dads) that met once a week with their children. The idea was for dads to hang out, discuss sports and parenting or whatever, and let the children play together. I loved the idea, and thought this would be the perfect scenario for Ryan to play with children his age and for me to bond with other SAHDs by getting some "normal" time with other guy's guys.

As much as I loved spending time with Ryan, I was growing tired of the only conversations I was having with my present company, which—when I could understand them (see chapter 4)—mainly revolved around Elmo and whether or not he had to use the potty. So I was thrilled with the idea of a SAHD group, and truly believed that whoever thought of it should be nominated for the Nobel Prize. Or at least given a free lap dance at the local strip club.

My SAHD group was the first of its kind where I live, and garnered some national attention. The group was featured on the TV show *CBS Sunday Morning* that year, and Ryan (obviously being the cutest kid in the group—not that I'm biased or anything) was featured prominently in the segment. (Incidentally, this was by far the best time I had with this group, and soon realized that it would be the highlight of my experience with them, and I pretty much quit going soon after this TV appearance. But I'm getting ahead of myself. . . .)

I was excited to be part of the group, and was equally excited that maybe now I could find some kinship—nay, brotherhood—in this group of manly men doing what was natural and for the good of our children.

But wouldn't you know it? What I experienced with the group and what I had hoped to experience with the group were two entirely different things, much to my dismay. I had imagined this group of cool guys hanging out, playing poker, talking about tits and ass while the kids played with each other quietly in a far-off distant room. In my imagination, there may even have been beer and Hooters girls involved. But I digress. In my delusional state, I had envisioned the other fathers and me opening the hood of one of the guys' muscle car and each of us pretending to understand the ins and outs of the motor, even though secretly we would be completely lost. The owner of the car would be saying things like, "Yeah, I went with the three-quarter-inch glass packs and gaffers on the manifold's spanktometer. It was a little more expensive, but the conglomerated steel-rod fibersnatchometers wouldn't make it through the harsh summer around here" or whatever. And we (the other guys who had no clue about this stuff and can barely fill our cars up with gas without consulting the manual, but still wanted to seem like we were worthy of our own testicles) would be saying, "No shit? Good idea. That's exactly what I'd do. In fact, I think I'm going to trick out my minivan once I get my tax refund, but first I gotta go flush out the bumper fluid." And we would all know that we were full of shit and as ignorant about cars as a monkey, but we'd celebrate this manly conversation by lighting up giant cigars and slapping each other on the back in a playful we-sure-are-cool manner. But as I said before, what I imagined would be the truth and what the experience was actually like were two completely separate things.

My first meeting was at the house of one of the key members of the group. He was hosting a pool party for the children, and the dads were to hang out and grill hot dogs.

This sounded like a great idea in theory. But when I got there, I could see things weren't going to go as I had imagined. All of the guys were dumpy, balding dudes who had yet to lose their sympathy baby weight. Their kids were all brats with enough combined snot hanging out of their noses to fill a gallon jug. The kids wouldn't play with each other, unless you count trying to drown the smaller children in the pool as playing together. And I don't. So I spent my time not bonding with the guys so much as I swam with my two-year-old and tried to fend off three-year-old tyrant bullies who wanted to ride my son's back like he was an inner tube with a pulse.

Once it was time to eat, we all sat down with our kids in our laps (so much for the kids-playing-quietly-in-the-other-room fantasy) and we sipped on juice boxes and ate charred hot dogs. And the conversation wasn't about cars, guns, sports, girls, or anything else I had envisioned. Instead they talked trash about whoever wasn't there at the time. It was like watching a bunch of little old ladies at the hairdresser gossip under the dryers.

SAHD 1: "Did you see Tom last week? What was with that outfit he was wearing?"

SAHD 2: "I know. And his hair is falling out at an alarming rate."

SAHD 3: "Tell me about it. You know, I hear his wife is screwing the intern at the major corporation where she is the CFO."

SAHD 1: "No!"

SAHD 3: "Yes!"

SAHD 2: "NO!"

SAHD 3: "YES!"

SAHD 1: "Well, I don't blame her. I hear he can't get it up anymore since he has been downing all of those antidepressants."

SAHD 2: "No!"

SAHD 1: "Yes!"

SAHD 3: "*No!*"

SAHD 1: "*Yes!* By the way, I love that diaper bag. It really brings out your eyes. Where did you get it?"

And there wasn't a goddamn Hooters girl within a twenty-mile radius.

I only attended one or two of these events before I realized that this wasn't for me. I was destined to be a lone SAHD without a group—a sad SAHD—and it really bummed me out. I was hoping for some comrades to help fight in this battle of stereotypes. I wanted the world to know that we were not just Mr. Mom: we were cool dudes in our thirties who, even though we change shitty diapers and speak baby talk a good portion of the day, were still men who could do manly things together. Instead I got to hang out with the cast of the all-male road-company version of *Steel Magnolias*.

I'm not trying to discourage anyone from bonding together in groups. I absolutely think a good SAHD group would be a marvelous thing, and a great opportunity for dads to get together and share their experiences with other fathers. I'm thinking of starting one now. We'd have it at the local Hooters, where we'd drink beer and smoke cigars, and any gossiping candy-ass bitch-boy would be shown the door so fast he wouldn't know what hit him. Then we'd discuss our kids, sports, hot women we had seen on TV or around town, and, of course, how much we love our nickel-plated flank-shafted carburetor bearings (whatever the hell *that* means).

End of Chapter Review Questions

What have we learned here?

1.   What is the meaning of the term *SAHD*?
     a. Sporting Association of Hunting Ducks

  b. Sullen Alcoholic Half-dead Dads
  c. Stay-At-Home Dads
  d. Sycophantic Assholes Hating Day Jobs: Dads who make excuses to their wives about how they'd be better stay-at-home parents and then spend the rest of their lives mooching off the wages earned by their hard-working wives (contributed by Julie Crider, for some unknown reason. . . . Hey, wait a minute. . . .).

2. What kind of corporation would hire Harriet Nelson as their CFO?

3. What intern in his right mind would want to see Harriet's unsheathed breasts?

4. Isn't it sad how little I actually know about cars?

5. HAVE YOU EVER NOTICED THAT WHEN PEOPLE TYPE IN ALL CAPS IT APPEARS THAT THEY'RE YELLING AT THE READER? HUH? HAVE YOU?

6

I Am Father, Hear Me Roar

FROM JACK, A REAL *GUY'S GUIDE* GUY:

For me, the most interesting thing about becoming a dad is that I totally lost my identity. I wasn't Jack anymore; I was "Daddy." It might as well have replaced my given name on my birth certificate and driver's license. And the truth of it was, I thought it was pretty cool. I didn't mind at all. Being a father is a lot of fun, except for the messy shit you have to deal with all the time. Aside from that, I dig it. The best is when my kids look at me like I'm a god or something like that. They think that I am this all-knowing guru of life who can fix their toys or answer any questions they have about the world. So I am this superhero guy to them, which is pretty cool. I don't look forward to the day when they become teens and see their old man as this dipshit loser who doesn't know his ass from his elbow. But then if my experience is any gauge they will get into their twenties and thirties and see that I wasn't so dumb after all.

As the father of a toddler, I am many things. I cannot be defined by one or two words. I, having accepted the role of "father," have also agreed to oversee certain duties and responsibilities. Although I have a real name, it has been replaced by *Daddy, Dad, Pops, Papa,* and *Bald Mommy,* among others, yet I answer to many other monikers. I'm like a superhero with many identities and personalities:

I am the chaser of the bogeyman.   I make sure my child can go to sleep in peace, knowing that the bad guys from the cartoon he was just watching are nowhere in sight.

I am the exterminator.   I kill baby spiders so tiny that they can only be seen with a microscope or the eyes of a frightened two-year-old.

I am the playmate.   It is my duty to lose to my child at every game—from checkers to wrestling to poker to video games.

I am the clown.   If my kid is scared or in pain, I will fall down, make funny faces, talk in silly voices, sing goofy songs, and trip over objects in an exaggerated manner just to make him laugh or forget his troubles.

I am the diaper changer and the potty trainer.   I've seen more poop and pee than a worker at the Newark sewage treatment plant.

I am the doctor.   I apply bandages and kisses to boo-boos when a scrape on the knee seems to bring the world to an end.

I am the punisher.   I seem larger than life and scary when my kid has done something wrong.

I am the chauffeur.   I take my son to school, the doctor's office, soccer games, the grocery store, "Elmo-on-Ice," and to see Santa Claus. And speaking of Santa Claus . . .

I am Santa Claus.   Shhh . . . don't tell.

I am the keeper of the remote control.   No one should fight me on this one. I don't care who you are. You'll lose. (And that goes for your mommy, too.)

I am the toy finder.   I'm the one who instructs my child to look under the cat's litter box if he's somehow misplaced his Star Wars action figure for the thirty-second consecutive time in one day; my child is continually amazed every time he finds out that the Toy Finder is right.

I am the teacher.   I show you all the important things in life. No, not the three R's. I teach the truly important things. I teach you how to play football; I teach you the names of everyone who's ever been on *The Simpsons;* and I teach you how to do "arm farts" and to belch the first few lines of the *Star Spangled Banner*.

I am the music expert.   I explain to you the finite nuances and differences between the genres "hard rock" and "heavy metal," and tell you in great detail why Sammy Hagar is better than David Lee Roth.

I am your maid.   I constantly clean up your messes, even after telling you repeatedly that I am not your maid and that I will no longer clean up your messes.

I am the world's biggest hypocrite.   Don't cuss, don't drink, don't smoke, don't do drugs, don't flunk out of college, don't eat shitty foods, and don't avoid vegetables at all cost. Do as I say, not as I do.

I am your chef.   I can open a can of Chef Boyardee like nobody's business and serve you your feast of spaghetti and meatballs in the blink of an eye.

I am the great contradictor.   I tell you to grow up and punish you for acting like the little kid you actually are, but then become greatly upset at the thought of you growing up and no longer needing me.

But most of all . . .

I am your father.   And don't you forget it.

End of Chapter Review Questions

What have we learned here?

1. Who am I? (No seriously, I'm asking. I wasn't trying to get you to say "You are Father" or anything. I honestly can't remember my name. I think I'm having a stroke. Please call for an ambulance.)

2. Do you think the male I-must-be-the-keeper-of-the-remote gene goes as far back as caveman days? Like maybe when the husband came home from a long day of hunting for saber-toothed tigers, he would sit down on his favorite reclining rock and try to change all the hieroglyphics on the wall of the cave until he saw his favorite buffalo picture?
    a. Yes
    b. No
    c. What the hell are you talking about?

Why aren't you calling an ambulance like I asked? Can't you see I'm not well?

7

Why Every Child in the World Sucks But Your Own

FROM DOUGLAS, A REAL *GUY'S GUIDE* GUY:

I try to be open-minded about other people's kids. I try to teach my kids that everyone is equal. No one is better than anyone else. I wanted to teach my kids this because I had a bigoted dad who believed that basically anyone who wasn't him or one of his friends was an idiot and barely human. So I wanted to teach my children that people were good for the most part, and that they should do their best to get along with everyone. But then I see these miserable little punks that are running around and I realize that I don't like kids. I only like MY kids. So maybe my father was onto something.

As my baby boy grew into his toddler phase with me as his only daily social interaction, I realized that it was time to get him out into the world and give him some playtime with other children his age. He needed the social time with his peers. He needed interaction with children his own age. And most importantly, he needed to get the hell out of my face.

See, as a stay-at-home dad, I get to spend a lot of quality time with my son. Some may even say too much quality time. And as we all know, you actually can have too much of a good thing. I was growing tired of being Ryan's only playmate, and was in the mood for some much-needed grown-up time myself. But getting this done would prove to be tricky. After all, I had already tried to bond with other stay-at-home dads at what turned out to be a support group for so-called men who had somehow turned into gossiping housewives, and that had proved to be a disaster. So I had to come up with other tactics and plans.

Every time I saw a "For Sale" sign in one of my neighbor's yards, I became filled with hope and excitement. Our neighborhood at the time was filled with kids, though most of those kids were too old to play with (or want to play with) a two-year-old. So each time one of our friends and/or neighbors would move, the thought that maybe, just maybe, someone Ryan's age would move in would get me interested. I was very optimistic that not only would the child be the same age as my son, but would also be a sweet, caring little person (like my son). I wanted someone Ryan could grow up with, have play dates with, spend the night with at a slumber party or whatever . . . you know, regular *Leave It to Beaver*–type children. This is what I had hoped would happen. And every once in a while, a child his age would move in. And inevitably, these children would be precisely the opposite of what I wanted. They were mean, nasty little bastards who were not going to be allowed anywhere near my little guy.

As the parent of a toddler, we all need to be honest with ourselves and readily admit that, for the most part, we don't really like anyone else's toddlers except our own. It's true. I know it, and you know it. You may be sitting there thinking, "That's not true. I love the toddler next door." And that's a nice sentiment. But it's also probably total and utter bullshit. You don't like other peoples' toddlers, and neither do I. OK, sure, there are exceptions. And to my close friends who are reading this thinking, "He doesn't like my kid?" I want you to know that you are the exception to this rule. If I didn't like your kid, I would find a reason not to hang out with you. (And for those thinking, "We don't hang out anymore. Does that mean he doesn't like my kid?" The answer is . . . probably.)

In general, other people's kids suck. The sooner you can admit this to yourself, the sooner you can move on and face reality. They're dirty, they spend half the day smelling like peanut butter and piss, they're germ-laden, they put your cat's tail in the VCR, they pick their ugly little pug noses and wipe the boogers on your brand-new high-definition television, they talk back, they don't listen, they scream at the top of their lungs, they hit both their friends and their parents alike, they bite your perfect little angel on the cheek just to try and get attention, they take your gold-fish out of its bowl and throw it against the wall just to see what would happen . . . they're awful people. They're miniature Satans. No. I take that back. I would like to apologize for that last remark, and wish for it to be stricken from the record, if it pleases the court at this time. That wasn't a fair statement. The truth is they're actually worse than Satan. At least Satan would have the good sense and manners to at least wipe the crumbs off of his mouth after eating that chocolate-chip cookie that he stole from your child's plate.

If somehow you happen to find a child worthy of play-ing with your own, then you have to find a family whose parents aren't total assholes. It's rare when you find that perfect combination of a child who has the right temperament to play with your own kid and who has parents that you can get along with. It's like when you try to find another married couple to hang out with when you're a couple: you usually like one of them, but think the other is a total douche bag. So if you find a child that you can actually stand and whose parents are able to carry on a conversation, grab these people and hold onto them for dear life. They're a rare find, like a rookie Mickey Mantle baseball card or a stripper who can count to ten. In fact, I think there needs to be some sort of screening system when you meet new people who have children your child's age. Think of what a time-saver that would be! Picture this scenario and then realize how much easier it would be if you had a pre-friendship application:

You and your child are playing at a nearby park. Your sweet little toddler says, "Daddy, watch me go down the slide," for the seven-hundredth time, and then gets scared when he's at the top looking down the chute for the seven-hundredth time and makes you climb up after him to get him down for the seven-hundredth time. At this point, some typical soccer mom walks up to you with that "my frosted and feathered helmet hair was cool back in 1989 and still is DAMMIT" looking mop on her head, a self-knitted sweater with an apple on it, her jeans riding too high on her belly that she never lost but still claims that it's her "baby weight" (even though her child is entering pre-school in a month), and on her feet are those white Keds shoes that somehow every soccer mom owns. She looks at you and says, "What a sweetie! How old is your son? Maybe he and my little (insert trendy name here) could play on the teeter-totter together."

Now you can tell just by looking at this yuppie and her child with the mushroom-cut hairdo, turtleneck shirt/cardigan sweater combo and penny loafer shoes that you are not going to like this family. Wouldn't it be great to hand them a piece of paper and say, "You know I would love to continue this conversation. But first, would you please fill out this application?" And the application, which could be customized and personalized to fit your specific needs, would follow the basic form of this example:

NAME:_____

ADDRESS:_____

CITY:_____

STATE:_____

PHONE NUMBER:_____

BIRTHDATE:_____

NAME OF CHILD:_____

AGE AND BIRTHDATE OF CHILD:_____

ARE YOU OR YOUR CHILD CONSIDERED AN ANNOYING ASSHOLE BY ANYONE IN YOUR IMMEDIATE FAMILY OR CIRCLE OF FRIENDS?_____

IF YOU ANSWERED "YES" TO THE "ANNOYING ASS-HOLE" QUESTION, PLEASE EXPLAIN.

_____

DOES YOUR CHILD HAVE A TRENDY NAME THAT YOU FELL IN LOVE WITH WHEN YOU WERE PREGNANT AND WATCHING AN EPISODE OF "THE GILMORE GIRLS" OR ANY OTHER DRAMATIC COMEDY (OR DRAMA-DY)?

_____

ON A REGULAR BASIS, DO YOU USE THE PHRASES "TOO MUCH INFORMATION," "DON'T GO THERE," "DRAMA-DY," OR WINK AND SAY "I'M JUST KIDDIN'" EVEN WHEN IT'S OBVIOUS TO EVERYONE IN THE WORLD THAT YOU'RE JUST KIDDING?_____

REFERENCES:_____

THANK YOU FOR APPLYING TO BE OUR FRIEND. PLEASE ALLOW FOUR TO SIX WEEKS FOR ONE OF OUR REPRE-SENTATIVES TO CONTACT YOU FOR THE FIRST IN A SERIES OF INTERVIEWS.

This really would make your life a lot easier. Sadly, these friendship applications do not exist just yet. They will. Someday. I promise. I contend that when I'm president of the United States, I will enforce the Homeland Friendship Security bill and you will be able to purchase these applications (on my Web site—at a very reasonable cost). And then no one will be forced to spend time with annoying assholes and/or the children of said assholes. But until then, you're stuck trying to feel out the parent and child who have approached you on the playground. And you will have to determine on your own if you want to spend every free minute of your social life with these people.

That's one thing you never anticipate when wanting your child to have friends. You never realize that not only are your children going to have to try and get along, but you're also going to have to spend an exorbitant amount of time with the kid's entire family. From birthday parties to play dates to swim parties . . . you're never going to get away from them. And the entire time you spend at these functions, you are thinking to yourself, "Maybe he doesn't need the social interaction. Friends are overrated anyway. . . . "

And perhaps they are. I mean, by allowing your child to play with other kids and have a social life, you start to lose control, the control over ever facet of your child's life you've enjoyed up until now. You realize that in wanting friends, your child, your *baby*, is not a baby anymore. He is open to outside influences, and that creates a situation where you are no longer in control of your child's every move. Whereas you may have taught your child that hitting is wrong, biting is wrong, talking back is wrong, or whatever, other parents aren't always that stringent when it comes to teaching their children right from wrong. So what ends up happening (or what you're afraid will be happening) is that your child, who was once this little angel who does nothing wrong, will come home after a play date with his friends and be a completely different person. The fear is that he'll have a tattoo that says, "Elmo Sucks" on his forearm. He'll have a pack of little candy cigarettes rolled up in his shirt sleeve. When you tell him to clean his room, he'll say, "You do it. You're the bitch around here, Mr. Mom." And then you'll have to kill him. And really, who wants that?

In my case, the truth is I wasn't really upset with the way Ryan's "friends" were behaving, or how their parents were useless masses of skin with no parental skills whatsoever. In reality, I was upset that I wasn't able to control the other kids' every move, and therefore wouldn't be able to control what my son would mimic and turn out to be. I was one step closer to losing my son to the influences of the rest of the world. Soon he would be . . . gulp . . . his own person.

End of Chapter Review Questions

What have we learned here?

1. What word best describes everyone else's children in the world but yours?
   a. Dirty
   b. Smelly
   c. Stupid
   d. Ugly
   e. Diseased
   f. All of the above

2. Why is it that some women go from "cool chick" to "I made my own clothes out of old expired coupons to save money and I think I look great" when they have children?

3. Why do kids always get to the top of the slide and then decide they can't make it down on their own? Let me get this straight: you were brave enough to climb twenty feet in the air on a ladder, but now I gotta climb my fat ass up there to help you slide down? (Clearly that was more of a rhetorical question than anything else.)

8

....

Party Animals

....

FROM LENNY, A REAL *GUY'S GUIDE* GUY:

When you find the one with whom you want to spend the rest of your life, there are many unexpected "events" that follow. Women never tell guys about these things because I am certain that they would be afraid that we would run away as fast we could if we knew about them all. After the wedding showers (and the coed ones—who the hell came up with those?) come the baby showers, which are pretty much the same drill as the wedding shower, just with different accessories. And believe me, there are some scary ones—diapers are the least of them. Then come the children themselves . . . and the birthday parties.

Chuck E. Cheese Hell—as I call it—is a room full of dozens of screaming, crying, sweaty children that are all strung out on birthday cake and Capri-Sun. Holy God, nothing could prepare you for this. And God help you if you ever host one of these events. It will cost ridiculous amounts of money. Not only is there pressure to have the coolest birthday party ever, but you must also buy "loot bags" full of little gifts for every child in attendance. That's the part I don't get. Wouldn't you think that I have been paying my dues all year by bringing a gift to everyone else's party? Sorry. The kid world does not work that way my friend. And there is nothing you can do to change that. In the end, is it all worth it? Of course it is. Just be warned friend, just be warned.

As I mentioned in the previous chapter, once you become the parent of a socially active toddler, you get many opportunities to hang out with the families of the other children your child becomes friends with. Your son or daughter acquires these friends through day care, classes, play dates, church functions, or maybe even singles bars for kids—places where they can enjoy juice boxes together and see if they can make a friend connection of some sort with another toddler. (In this day and age, you *know* there has to be at least one of those types of clubs. And they're probably based in California. Just a guess.) The point is, you will be forced to spend time with other families because of their association to your child. So you strap your kid into his or her car seat and drive them to the house of whatever function you're being forced to go to. Sometimes these events are pool parties. Sometimes they're Christmas parties. Later they'll be bar mitzvahs, bat mitzvahs, and funerals (if you're lucky; they always have good finger foods at funerals), but most of the time you'll be dragging your family out to the birthday party of one of the kids your child calls "friend."

Allow me to explain why I put quotation marks around the word *friend*. Toddlers don't really choose the people they hang around with. Not that I'm saying that the children don't have the capacity to decide who they like and who they dislike. But for the most part, they're around whom we want them to be around at any given time and will play with them simply because there is no real alternative. Whereas when I think of adults having friends, I think of the people we have bonded with over time who have similar interests, senses of humor, and whatnot; kids just play with whomever we tell them to. And it's a good bet that toddlers in particular will like anyone or anything that is funny, makes gross noises, or is shiny. They don't need this to be another toddler.

Frankly, a toddler would consider a plastic toy chimp that farts when you squeeze it a close friend and confidant. It's not as if they're overly choosy as to whom they break bread with. But since we need to define and distinguish the identities of these other children your toddler is hanging around with, we'll just use the term "friend" for now. Just so long as we all understand the difference here.

Back to the friend's party. Yes, inevitably the parents of this new friend deem it necessary to celebrate the anniversary of the day that this precious little bastard shot out of his mother's crotch, and I'm forced to spend my Saturday afternoon at this kid's party.

When going to a birthday party for one of Ryan's fellow toddlers, aka friends, we—Julie and I—had to decide what kind of present to get the other child. If this friend happened to be a girl, Julie was in luck. Julie liked shopping for little girls because this gave her the opportunity to buy girly toys or clothes, something she didn't get to do very often for me and Ryan. And for girls there is an infinite variety of potential presents. Julie knows how to pick 'em. I could have bought these girls a huge diamond ring and a gift certificate for a free leg waxing, but that might have been considered inappropriate.

When it came time to shop for a boy, we ran into the inevitable dilemma of "What the hell does this kid have and what does he need?" For boys, there is precious little variety available.

You see, first-time parents usually shower their children with gifts (as we did with Ryan) and therefore the birthday boy usually already has everything his little heart desires. So the combination of not knowing what to give the boy and not wanting to spend a lot of money on a gift for a kid we didn't know very well led us to do something that, although I'm not particularly proud of this, proved to be a great solution. We would go through Ryan's closet, find a present given to him that he had no interest in or had completely forgotten about, and we would (as they said on a classic *Seinfeld* episode) "re-gift." For those of you unaware of the term *re-gift*, it generally means that you take something that was given to you as a gift and you simply hand it off to someone else as a gift specifically chosen and bought for them. This may seem like a thoughtless and callous thing to do to someone. But we Criders like to think of it as an earth-friendly thing to do, kind of like recycling. After all, if you weren't going to make use of the gift given to you, perhaps someone else would. And re-gifting is not that uncommon of a practice. After all, how many fruit-cakes have you received from your grandmother at Christmastime that somehow ended up going to your boss at your annual office party? Be honest.

After choosing the perfect gift (by closing our eyes and randomly grabbing the first intact/relatively unused thing we found in Ryan's closet) we would trek out to the local Chuck E. Cheese's, We Backwards-R Kids, Bouncy Jumping Place, or the public pool to join the birthday party. I don't know why, but all kid parties are held in places like this, and they're all pretty much interchangeable. Maybe there are manuals out there suggesting to the reader that they all hold their parties in similar venues. I don't know. Perhaps there is some sort of *Guy's Guide to Kid's Birthday Parties* that I don't know about. (But in case there isn't, don't even think about trying to write it. I'm filing the copyright paperwork now. . . .)

These parties are generally all the same, and are for the most part completely interchangeable from the last one, probably a party we attended the week prior. If you're a toddler birthday party virgin, here's the drill at your average store-bought, theme shindig: The kid whose birthday it is, whose name is probably something like Conner or whatever name was hip at the time of the pregnancy, has a bunch of kids in the room running around like banshees. As the other guests and their parents enter the venue that Conner's parents have paid a small fortune in which to host their precious angel's birthday party, they all go running into a large room with a large amount of balloons and colorful blinking lights. These rooms usually have loud arcade games that whistle or clang or have laser sounds and blaring, fast-tempo music that immediately cause the children to launch into an overstimulated state of mind. Their manic states are usually compounded by the large quantities of sugar given to them by the hosts in the form of candy in a "gift bag," and they soon enter into hyperdrive mode that they won't come down from until the following Tuesday.

Sometimes these facilities have large inflatable cages for the children to go into and bounce around. These contraptions are really just head injuries waiting to happen. They are huge rubber air mattresses that are being fed through an enormous fan underneath, and are incredibly taut and bouncy. They have a thin layer of netting around the perimeter to keep the children from falling out, or even escaping if they want to. There is just a tiny tent-like flap for an opening in which you deposit your child and allow them to jump around for hours on end. The kids laugh, scream, and chase each other in their stocking feet until they are all out of breath and the sugar high wears half off. This all seems like fun and games until one child falls, and the other sixty children crammed into this torture chamber begin trampling on the fallen child. Crying ensues, you begin to hear "Stop! Stop! You're hurting me! My spleen is hanging out of my anus! DADDY, HELP!" and it becomes like the 1979 concert by The Who in Cincinnati, in which eleven people were crushed to death by others in the crowd. Then when you finally are able to dig through the dog pile of kids and can drag your child out by his one un-broken limb, you kiss his boo-boos and ask if he's OK. In-evitably his answer will be, "I'm fine. Can I go again?" Toddlers are a weird bunch, man.

Then it comes time for Conner the birthday brat . . . uh . . . I mean, um boy to make a wish and blow out the candles on his cake. After fifteen minutes of concentrating on a wish, he tries to blow out the candles. For some rea-son, toddlers can never extinguish the candles the first time around, even if there are only one or two of them on the cake. Normally I wouldn't think this would be a difficult task, but what do I know? I'm not sure if maybe their aim is off, or if they just don't have strong enough lungs to han-dle the job. But as the child stands there turning red-faced and faint from the attempt, all I can think of is the fact that my elderly grandmother has a better lung capacity and could blow the candles out faster than these children. Any-way, the birthday boy finally puts out the candles, but not before he blows with more force than a tornado, sending approximately five gallons of spittle all across the top of the now-disease-ridden birthday cake. Then one of the soccer-mom mothers with the self-knitted apple sweater cuts the cake and divvies it up among the children, spreading joy and dozens of cases of the flu to the surrounding suburbs from the bacteria-laden frosting.

It ain't over yet.

Once the children's eyes become dilated from the sugar rushing to their brains, some genius (soccer mom) suggests that the birthday boy should open his presents from his "friends." Usually the birthday child is too timid to open the gifts and hides behind his mommy's leg as he begs and pleads for her to open the gifts for him. The mother then makes a deal with the child that she'll help him open the presents, but he has to sit up straight, smile, and say thank you for each gift. The birthday boy then proceeds to open each gift, toss it to the side without so much as a "thank you" or "kiss my ass," and moves on to the next present. In fact, the only emotion the child will show is when he looks the gift giver right in the eye and says, "I already have this," causing the parent of the gift giver to smile through gritted teeth and say, "Oh, That's OK. We weren't sure if he had that or not. You know, I do so love the honesty of children. Isn't that cute. . . . "

At some point, I will hear the mother say, "Oh this one is from your friend Ryan. You know Ryan, right?" and the child looks around the room with a bewildered look on his face. He doesn't know Ryan. Ryan doesn't know him, either. We're just there because one time six months ago Julie or I accidentally introduced ourselves to the parents at a "Sesame Street Live" concert, and now we were forced to go to this goddamn party and pretend to like these people. So no, of course he doesn't know Ryan. But by God they're "friends."

Anyway, the child opens the present that we so thoughtfully plucked from Ryan's closet and holds it up for his mother to see. The mother will then inevitably say, "Oh, a Transformer toy that turns from a fire-breathing robot to Hillary Clinton. I think we got Ryan one of these for his birthday last month." Oops. Busted. But to avoid looking like the guilty re-gifters we are, Julie and/or I just smile and say, "Well, he loved it so much that we thought your son would love it, too." And the whole time that we're lying, Julie and I are each hoping against hope that the other one remembered to take off the tag that says, "Happy Birthday Ryan. From your friend, Conner."

Eventually these parties do thankfully come to a close, and you'll get to leave with your hyper child who now has a bellyache and is inches away from losing a foot to diabetes from eating too much crap. You'll go home—as we always do—exhausted, but taking comfort in the knowledge that you only have six or seven more of these parties to go to in the next week.

End of Chapter Review Questions

What have we learned here?

1. What is the best method for saving money on a birth-day present for your child's "friend"?

   a. Make the gift yourself.

   b. When you get to the party, knock the tag off of someone else's present and write your child's name in where the other kid's name used to be.

   c. Print a certificate you made on your home computer that says, "A donation was made in your brat's name to the local office of Planned Parenthood."

2. What is your definition of a "friend"?

   a. A lifelong companion who shares interest with you and stays with you through thick and thin.

   b. Someone who your mother makes you play with and makes you go to their birthday parties.

   c. A douche bag who comes over to your house, eats all your food, drinks all your beer, and then hits on your wife.

9

Santa Claus Is Comin' to Town

FROM CORY, A REAL *GUY'S GUIDE* GUY:

Last year, my youngest (who is three) went through a phase where he was scared to death of Santa. When we went to the mall to have all four kids sit on Santa's lap and tell him what they wanted for Christmas, he freaked out. He screamed and cried. It was kind of embarrassing, but hysterically funny. So I knew I was running a risk by showing up at our house wearing my Santa Claus outfit, my annual holiday tradition. But I thought that if he saw Santa in his house, he would know that it was nothing to be scared of and he would get over his fear. Instead, when he saw me walk through the front door with my Santa suit on, he ran over to me, screamed "Die, bastard!" and punched me right in the balls. After that I didn't play Santa anymore, and my kid learned what soap tasted like. I literally made him suck on a bar of soap like that kid on A Christmas Story, *and he has never used the word bastard since that day.*

Fewer things about parenting excite me more than Christmastime. I love Christmas, and I always have. Ever since I can remember, I've always felt that there was a powerful and magical feeling about the entire Christmas season. No matter what was going on in my life as a child, no matter if I had been sick or had been having trouble in school, Christmas solved all of my problems. I loved the whole concept of Christmas, and I still love it all: the chill in the air (provided you live north of the old Manson/Nixon line), the smell of turkey cooking in the oven for our Christmas feast, the way my neighbors decorate their houses with lights and goofy little inflatable Rudolphs (OK, I can't pawn that off on my neighbors. . . . I'm actually the one who does that), the electricity in the air that you can feel when family comes together for the first time all year, the way Julie gets drunk on whiskey-spiked eggnog and lets me have my way with her . . . all of it.

But the one thing I love about Christmas the most is the look on my son's face when he wakes up and sees what Santa has left him on Christmas morning. There is no other feeling like that on the planet, and it fills me with joy. It also takes me back to the way I felt about Christmas as a child. And is there anything better than that feeling? (Well, actually there is. Eggnog-induced sex is pretty awesome. But I digress. . . .)

As much as I love Christmas, Santa hasn't been a big part of the mystique for me and Julie felt the same way. Before we had Ryan, we agreed that we would not perpetuate the Santa myth. It seemed wrong to lie to our child and fill his head full of fantasies about a fat man squeezing down the chimney and leaving presents for him and every other child in the world in just one night. We both remembered what a disappointment it was when we found out the truth about Santa. And no way were we going to bring that kind of disappointment to our son. But then something happened (I find I've written that phrase several times already. . . . could this be a theme? Discuss amongst yourselves) we had our baby, and the fun of the season took over. Before long, we were talking to Ryan about Santa, reading books about Santa, telling him that if he was a good little boy Santa would bring him lots of presents . . . it was all Santa systems go. And although we both knew we were setting our toddler up for an eventual mind-crippling disappointment, we also knew that he was loving every second of the illusion while it lasted.

Truth be told, Santa is not only a fun fantasy to get wrapped up in; he's also a very effective and powerful figurehead when it comes to rearing your children. Never underestimate the threat of Santa's vengeance against children who were misbehaving all year round. This is a tactic that has been handed down in my family for generations. My parents used to hold Christmas over my head as a way to keep me from getting into trouble. If I was acting like a jackass in say, July, all that my mom had to say was, "Santa's watching you, and is going to give you nothing but coal in your stocking if you don't straighten up," and I'd immediately change my attitude. The threat of coal in the stocking was enough to send me into fits for six months. Eventually, Christmas Eve would roll around, and I'd be lying sleeplessly in my bed, my little four-year-old mind thinking frantically, "Am I going to get coal in my stocking tomorrow morning? I really acted like an asshole a few times this year." Inevitably, I would wake up the next morning to find a cornucopia of gifts, and I would be re-

lieved to know that I once again cheated fate and fooled
the fat man again.

Knowing that my parents tortured me with the intimi-
dating thought of Santa opening a can of whoop-ass on my
four-year-old little frame, I had decided that I would not
do that to Ryan. I didn't want to threaten him with coal or
dog shit in his stocking. I wanted him to go to bed on
Christmas Eve and be excited—not worried—for the next
day's events. But then when he turned two years old, he
was acting like—how should I put this lightly and lovingly?—a total horse's ass. He was being a typical two-year-
old, saying no when I asked him to do something,
throwing fits—all the shit that goes along with being a toddler. So what did I do? I whipped out the old, "If you're
bad, Santa won't bring you any presents" lie that had been
passed on from generation to generation. And much to my
surprise, it rendered the boy helpless. He surrendered.
There was nothing he wanted more than to keep Santa
happy. A happy Santa all year means a happy boy on
Christmas Day. I dread the day when Ryan comes to the
realization that the whole Santa Claus thing is a farce.
Knowing the way his little scientific mind works, he'll
probably come up to me with a list of reasons why he believes he had been duped for all those years. I imagine the
confrontation will go something like this:

Dad, I have compiled a list of reasons why Santa is fake and I can prove—beyond a shadow of a doubt—that you've been lying to me ever since I was a baby. First of all, Santa has thirty-one hours of Christmas to work with, thanks to the different time zones and the rotation of the earth, assuming he travels east to west (which seems logical). This works out to 822.6 visits per second. This is to say that for each visited household with good children, Santa has 1/1000th of a second to park, hop his fat white ass out of the sleigh, jump down the chimney, fill the stockings, distribute the presents under the tree, eat whatever sugar-filled and cholesterol-laden snacks have been left, get back up the chimney, get back to the sleigh, and move on to the next house. Assuming that each of these 91.8 million stops are evenly distributed around the planet, we are now talking about 0.78 miles per household, a total trip of 75.5 million miles, not counting stops to do what most of us must do at least once every thirty-one hours (sleep, drink, take a dump, etc.), plus feeding the exhausted reindeer and all that stuff. This means that Santa's sleigh is moving at 650 miles per second, 3,000 times faster than the speed of sound. And don't let's forget the payload on the sleigh and how it adds another interesting element. Assuming that each child gets nothing more than a medium-sized Lego set (two pounds), the sleigh is carrying 321,000 tons, not counting Santa. On land, conventional reindeer can pull no more than three-hundred pounds. Even assuming that "flying reindeer" (which is complete and utter bullshit; I'll get to that later) could pull *ten times* the normal amount, we need 214,200 reindeer. This increases the payload—not even counting the weight of the sleigh—to 353,430 tons, or roughly four times the weight of Rush Limbaugh. So that's 353,000 tons traveling at 650 miles per second, creating enormous air resistance heating the reindeer up in the same fashion as spacecraft reentering the earth's atmosphere. This means that the lead pair of reindeer will absorb 14.3 *quintillion* joules of energy per second. Basically, they will burst into flame almost instantaneously, exposing the reindeer behind them, and create deafening sonic booms in their wake. The entire reindeer team would be vaporized within 4.26 thousandths of a second. Santa, meanwhile, would be subjected to centrifugal forces 17,500.06 times greater than gravity. A 250-pound Santa (which I'm estimating here for the purposes of this example) would be pinned to the back of the sleigh by 4,315,015 pounds of force. Now, let me ask you something, Dad. If I lied to you about something of that magnitude, wouldn't I get grounded? What else have you lied to me about? The Tooth Fairy? The Easter Bunny? For Christ's sake, is there anything you haven't lied to me about?

God, I dread that day. And at the rate his little mind is growing, I fear that day is not far away. But until then, I'll keep up the Santa illusion and hope for the best. After all, is there anything more fun than Christmas?

The entire Christmas season is magical. Even a severe pessimist such as yours truly gets a warm and fuzzy feeling during December. And even though it was fun before we had our son, it has been infinitely more fun since he was born. (Although if I'm being truthful, the first Christmas with our son was kind of lame. He didn't really know what was going on. He was too young to care about Santa, presents, and everything else that goes along with Christmastime. Hell, I bought his presents right in front of him at the store with him riding in the seat of the shopping cart. I think I even wrapped a couple of his presents while he was in the same room. He just had no clue.)

When he became a toddler, the fun really began. Ryan started to understand the entire concept of the entire gift-giving and receiving thing, and I began to see the look of anticipation in his eyes that I recalled from being a child his age some thirty years earlier.

Taking a child to see Santa Claus at the local mall is possibly one of the most fun events you can participate in as a parent. It's not only fun for the child to see this godlike figure in person, but it's fun for the adults to witness as well. The look in your toddler's eye when he or she rounds the corner and sees Santa is worth all the bad things you've been part of as a parent: the messy diapers, the vomit, the back talk, the frustrating crying-all-night-for-no-real-reason phase . . . suddenly that all goes away. And as a parent, you're now left with just a huge grin on your face because you are seeing your child's true happiness. For a child to see Santa in the flesh must generate the same sort of awe-inspired feeling that we as adults get when we see our favorite rock star or movie star. To a toddler, Santa is this larger-than-life personality who makes the impossible happen in this mysterious and miraculous way, and now to see him in a public place like in front of a JC Penney's or something must be a complete mind trip for a first-timer. Little boys are screaming "You rock, dude!" and holding autograph books, the toddler girls are lifting their Hello Kitty shirts and shouting, "Santa, I want to have your Cabbage Patch Kids" . . . it's bedlam. In a good way. I think these kids have a similar reaction that my wife would have if George Clooney were sitting in the middle of the mall and allowing fans to sit on his lap.

(As a quick side note here . . . at any other time in the year if you were in the mall and some strange man asked your child to come sit on his lap, you'd call the police. But give him a white beard and a red suit during the final month of the fiscal year, and suddenly it's OK somehow. Go figure.)

Except if they don't react that way. And usually they don't because we parents have wound our kids up into such a frenzy and we have unwittingly made our kids terrified of the big fat red-clad man. We sweat nervously as we try to get our children to sit up straight, tell Santa what they want, and smile nicely for the picture. Some parents—not Julie and I; I'm talking about the silly ones who overdo all holidays—act as if Santa will bypass their house if the kids don't say and do the right things. And as a result, the child—who was very excited at the idea of doing this at first—is now utterly freaked out. Santa asks what the little child wants, the child inevitably forgets due to nervousness, and the mother is doing that loud-whisper thing from the sidelines: "Tell him you want a new train and a video game! Tell him! Go on. Tell him! *Oh*, and don't forget the big-screen plasma television and new Lexus SUV for Mommy."

Then the child gets even more scared, decides this isn't going well and needs to end, and starts wiggling and wanting down off of the fat man's lap. The mother, in her high-rise "mom jeans," self-knitted reindeer sweater (she changed out of her self-knitted apple sweater for just this occasion) and Santa hat covering her frosted helmet hair, will say "No, no, no. Sit still while Mommy takes your picture" as she hopes against hope that her now-Prozac-needing child will smile a big, beautiful grin for the keepsake photo that they want to send out for this year's Christmas card. Instead, the end result is a glossy 8 x 10 of the little kid crying their eyes out with a snot bubble protruding from their nose, their mouth contorted like Sylvester Stallone calling for Adrienne at the end of *Rocky* and, in the center of the picture, a big wet spot on Santa's lap where the frightened child pissed all over their hero. Then one of Santa's helpers gives the permanently traumatized child a candy cane to make it all better, the next child walks up for their turn, and the cycle starts all over again. Rinse and repeat.

Once the tears, piss, and snot have all dried from the stressful Santa excursion, it's all over but the waiting. Christmas Eve usually finds the Criders at home reading Christmas books to our toddler and watching the old Claymation Christmas specials on television, *Rudolph, the Red-Nosed Reindeer* being our household favorite. Then as little

Ryan is tucked snugly into his little toddler bed, Santa goes into action. But this "Santa" doesn't come sliding down the chimney with a big sack of presents on his back, laying them all out magically and with all of the presents put together and perfectly wrapped. No, no. That's not the way it happens in this house. *This* Santa spends the next hour and a half dragging heavy shit in through the garage, pissed off and cussing his lungs out because "the goddamn toy manufacturer in Hong Kong printed the assembly instructions in a manner that even Einstein couldn't figure out."

Now granted, I'm not even remotely a handyman. To me, a screwdriver is a concoction made from vodka and orange juice. I am, if I'm being honest here, a pretty pathetic excuse for a man. I'm not even close to having that "fixer-upper" talent that my own father has. My dad can fix anything. Give him a single 2 × 4, a paper clip, and a wad of chewing gum, and he could somehow manage to make an entire apartment complex for homeless people—and do a perfect job of it in about twenty minutes. In contrast, I tried to make a squirrel feeder once, and the local office of HUD condemned it after three unsuspecting squirrels died during an unfortunate event where it collapsed and fell off of the tree. So when it comes to assembling toys whose boxes brag they are "Easy to Assemble," I'm pretty much useless.

And these are the times when my wife and I usually get into our worst arguments. As any married couple knows, the biggest fights always stem from the smallest things, usually involving something that is supposed to be sweet and fun, like vacations, birthday parties, or even Christmas. It always starts out the same way. Both of us, our intentions equally good, get excited that our toddler is going to have so much fun on Christmas morning, and we want to get the toys put together for him so he can immediately begin enjoying them. Then I drag in all the parts from the garage, and assess the assembly instructions of the first toy out of the hundred or so that need to be put together. Inevitably I can't seem to find the last screw that I need to finish the project and suddenly the whole world goes to hell. Julie and I start snapping at each other, we begin blaming the other one for losing the last screw, the name-calling begins, and then the threats of divorce and a murder/suicide pact begin. It never fails. Then finally one of us will exclaim something like, "Merry Friggin' Christmas to all, and to all you can kiss my ass! I'm going to bed! And I may not be here when you wake up tomorrow!" And then the other one is left alone downstairs to finish the toy-building process, usually finishing just before our son wakes up the next morning.

But all of that frustration and hostility falls by the wayside when our sweet little toddler wakes up in the morning to the realization that it is Christmas, and he wants to see what booty his good deeds for the year have rendered. The joy in his eye as he comes downstairs and sees the toys lined up underneath the tree is worth all of the trouble and hassle that comes along with the season. And once he rips all of the wrapping paper from the presents and says "Wow! Santa got me just what I wanted!" after each and every opened gift, he always does what children have done for centuries past: He plays with the empty boxes that the toys came in. Five thousand dollars worth of toys are lying still and lifeless on the floor and our sweet little toddler is making a tiny apartment out of the containers in which they came.

Out of all the things I miss about the baby and toddler stage, memories of playing Santa and seeing the look on my little boy's face on Christmas morning will be the most missed, by far. Once Ryan is old enough to start figuring out that these things don't quite add up, I'm going to be really bummed. But until then, I will keep on playing the pissed-off, cussing Santa. And it will always be worth it.

End of Chapter Review Questions

What have we learned here?

1. What's the best way to get a toddler to behave for 364 days out of the year?
   a. Tell him that Santa will not bring him any presents on Christmas.
   b. Threaten to take his favorite toys away until he behaves.
   c. Have him wake up one morning with Rudolph's severed head in bed with him, à la *The Godfather*.

2. What's the most effective way to get toddler pee stains out of a Santa outfit?

3. Why do people with the ugliest children insist on sending out Christmas cards with pictures of the offending child on them? Don't they know their kid's face looks like an elephant's butt?

4. Seriously, how much would you give to see a reindeer burst into flame and create a sonic boom? Wouldn't that be awesome?

5. Isn't it interesting how I have the ability to dread future separation anxieties like Ryan no longer believing in Santa? I really need to get a hobby.

6. What the hell is "nog," anyway? And why is it only served during the Christmas season? I have a sneaking suspicion that it's elf semen, so I think I'll just stay away from it altogether.

10

····································

Who's That
Sleeping in My Bed?

····································

FROM JOHN, A REAL *GUY'S GUIDE* GUY:

Whenever one of my kids has a nightmare or when it storms at night, they end up in my bed. They always ask if they can sleep with us. Usually I don't mind. But one night my wife and I were bumping uglies when our daughter had a bad dream and wanted to come into our bedroom for the rest of the night. She came bursting into the room with tears in her eyes and said she heard a ghost screaming outside of her bedroom door. When we heard the door to our bedroom open, we both jumped and squirmed around in the bed and pretended that we were sleeping instead of doing what we were actually doing. When my wife told her that she was just having a bad dream and should go back to bed, my daughter said "No, I really heard it. I wasn't asleep or nothing when I heard the ghost screaming." We asked her what the ghost was screaming and she said, "The ghost was screaming Oh God, Oh God over and over again." It was all we could do to keep from busting out laughing because we realized the sounds she was hearing were coming from our bedroom activities. I wrapped a blanket around my naked body and went downstairs to sleep on the couch while my daughter and her mother slept soundly in my bed all night long. After that we made sure we locked the bedroom door and tried to keep our late-night lovemaking as quiet as possible.

No surprise here, folks: when Ryan was an infant, getting him to go to sleep on his own was one of the most difficult tasks to master. From the very beginning, he liked to be held and rocked to sleep, whether it was time for him to take a nap during the day or when it was time for him to drift off to slumber land at night.

I'm assured by experts that this is not all that unusual. Most infants find it difficult to lie down and pass out on their own. There is a certain element of separation anxiety that sets in with most babies, and they don't want to be left alone. I don't know if they think they're going to miss something really cool while they sleep or maybe they think a party is going to spontaneously break out while they're napping, and somehow they're going to miss out on the fun. Or maybe they just don't want to be away from us parents, and so they don't want to fall asleep. Or all of the above.

For the first couple of months of my son's life, nap time and bedtime went like this: I paced around the room holding Ryan tight in my arms, gently rocking him while singing songs to him (usually "Beautiful Boy" by John Lennon, if you must know . . . nothing can beat that song. . . . It's a wonderful lullaby and love song Lennon wrote for his son Sean, and really speaks about the love between a father and his baby boy. Now I feel I need to redeem my manhood, so let me just say this: that song kicks ass!)

After singing proved to be an exercise in futility, my next step was to put him in his baby swing—which was near/in the kitchen—and turn on the dishwasher. But this, too, rarely worked (though I must say we had the cleanest dishes—and the largest water bill—in the entire neighborhood). In the end, what usually ended up happening was this: I would somehow find myself lying down with my baby boy on my own bed and staying there with him until he fell asleep. This was the only strategy that worked. Sometimes I'd then tiptoe out of the room to go watch some good TV (he couldn't even roll over yet—there was no danger in leaving him without crib bars around him, if that's what you're thinking). Sometimes—even during the day—I'd end up falling asleep right there with him. And sooner or later (later, rather than sooner I guess I should say) Ryan would float off to a place where nipples and brightly colored toys sang the ABCs to him. (I'm just guessing as to what he dreamed about, of course. There is no real way for me to actually know what his dreams involved. But let's face it: with his limited life experience, what more could he possibly have to dream of?) I can't say that my dreams were much more adventurous—hey, come to think of it . . . a land of singing nipples sounds pretty cool.

Finally, at a routine well-baby visit with our pediatrician, we were advised to stop being a crutch to little Ryan, and to start trying to make him fall asleep on his own, without the aid of willing (and exhausted) parents. The doctor said this was a vital step in Ryan's development, and necessary for us to ultimately regain sanity in our household (not to mention the privacy of our marital bed!). To be honest, I was glad for the doctor's orders: I no longer really wanted to spend the better part of my day fighting our son over mattress space. And remember, I was technically "working at home" during this time; I really needed Ryan to sleep on his own so that I could actually get some writing done. The bad news was that since I was the stay-at-home parent, I was going to have to be the one to enforce this new law. So one day at the normal nap time, I simply carried Ryan into his room, laid him down in his crib, and left. (And by "left," I mean I just left the room. It's not like I went to a bar and got hammered, leaving my son behind. The thought occurred to me, but I didn't do it.)

Of course, my baby boy immediately started crying, understandably not understanding why I had abandoned him. While he cried, I ran into our bedroom, covered my head with a pillow and said over and over again, "I'm sorry, Ryan. This is for your own good. I'm sorry, Ryan. This is for your own good." Within a matter of minutes, he had cried himself to sleep and I was able to get some work done, feeling guilty but at the same time knowing in my heart that this was the best thing for him. And being the awesome kid he was and still is, he took to this new routine very quickly. We only had to go through the separation-anxiety cry a couple of times before he finally got the hang of it and realized that either his daddy or his mommy would be there when he woke up. And I was very proud of him.

I know what you're thinking—that was too easy.

Fast-forward to Ryan's third year on the planet. Up until this time, he had been sleeping soundly in his own crib, both at nap time and at bedtime, and his mother and I had been sharing our marital bed as we had been for over a decade. We had all settled into this nice routine, and family life had become easier than when he was a newborn. It was all like second nature to us now. And then one night we heard a horrible noise coming from the baby monitor in his room. (Yes, even though he was now no longer an infant, we still had the monitor—I don't know how parents ever give this thing up, do you? We still use it. When the day comes that it's been dropped one too many times and doesn't work anymore, I'll run out and buy a new one. Until that kid turns twenty-one, I need to hear him breathing and talking in his sleep!)

Ryan began throwing up. I'm talking violent, projectile vomiting before which I had only seen on *The Exorcist*. It was awful. Some nasty germ had gotten its claws into our son and, though we didn't know it that night, would go on for months. Yes, Ryan threw up every fifteen minutes for months, and it was all we could do not to go insane. No doctor could tell us what was wrong, and he became so dehydrated from the constant vomiting that he was admitted to the hospital on more than one occasion.

At first, Julie and I took turns sleeping on Ryan's floor, but we soon realized that as effective as it was to be there to be able to reach out and hold a bucket in front of him at the first sign of vomit, bringing him to us—in our bed, where things were considerably more comfortable—was the way to go. Actually, we brought him to Julie. Remember, Ryan was now three—he needed more space than he had when he was a non-rolling infant. Suffice to say he slept with Julie, and I slept on the couch. After what seemed like an eternity, Ryan's stomach got back to normal and he was able to live like every other three-year-old, thank God. We were glad to have things back to the way they were, but mostly we were just thankful that our baby boy was feeling better. The problem was that now he was used to sleeping with his mommy, his mommy was used to sleeping with him, and I was still on the damn couch.

Looking back I can see that this sleeping arrangement was a metaphor for the way our house operated. We were "good" parents—involved, concerned, obsessed—and our lives necessarily revolved around our son's. We put his needs first, sometimes to the detriment of our marriage and relationship. It's not that we weren't getting along or that we weren't the same strong married couple we had been for over a decade. But now our roles had changed from a "couple" to a "family," and most of the time our needs as a couple took a backseat to our needs as a family. Let's put it this way: We have a print of John Lennon's painting *Two Is One*. Now one of us really should have reached up and scratched "Two" with a Sharpie. We had become "Three Is One." That's a nice sentiment and hey, it might not have been such a bad thing (for me) if the third wasn't also a guy and related to us, you know what I'm saying? But seriously, we sort of lost our needs as a couple in the process of tending to Ryan's.

Let me just say here for clarity purposes that I have no doubt in my mind that Julie, my lovely Asian war bride, loves me. She's seen me through good times and bad, but even when the times were tough, there was still a bond between us that has kept us going. She has her bad days, and God knows she deserves a medal for putting up with me for so long. But the fact remains that neither of us could fathom spending our lives with anyone else. So as I stated, I have no doubt that this woman loves me. That being said, I also know that the moment she laid eyes on her baby boy was also the same moment that I took a backseat to her love for her son. There is an unwritten and largely unspoken rule around here that in creating our son, I subsequently created my own replacement. Julie lives and breathes for that little guy, as do I. And if it all came down to it, if you asked her to choose between anyone in the world and her son, the rest of the world would lose. And that includes me now. If I ever said anything like, "Look, woman. This house isn't big enough for the three of us. So either he goes or I go," I'd be writing this book from deep inside my brand-new cardboard mansion underneath a bridge somewhere. And that's as it should be. I think any good parent knows that no one and nothing comes before the wants and needs of your child. But this creates a different kind of separation anxiety for the third wheel, a marital separation anxiety. And sadly, I found it doesn't end once the baby becomes a toddler.

As you may already know—or will soon find out—being the parent of a toddler is somewhat exhausting. They have a tendency to run you ragged. They constantly want attention and need something from their parents. I, for instance, would go from playmate to chef to doctor to VCR technician in the blink of an eye. Working for a magazine from my home office at the time, I also had writing deadlines and editors to appease. I was all things to all people at that time in my life. I was inevitably very tired by the time Julie got home from work in the evening. Desperate to get a few things checked off my own to-do list, I would hand off our son to his mother and get crackin'.

For her part, Julie was feeling guilty that she had to work all day and didn't get to spend the time with her son that she so desired and needed. So when she came home each evening, she would gladly take Ryan off of my hands. The problem was that it was like we were changing shifts at a factory or something. I'd finish my day shift, and she would come home and take the night shift. We'd merely pass each other at the time clock when we were punching in and out, nod to each other and go about our business. What was our first priority—Ryan—had soon become our only priority. And that, we learned, was not a good thing.

It's easy to get lost in the parental role and somehow forget who you once were before your child arrived. For over a decade before we were parents, we were always known as "Mike and Julie." It was almost as if it were one word, "MikeandJulie." We were always together. If you saw one of us, chances are you saw both of us. If there was a party, we were there together. If one of us was invited out to dinner, we were both there. We even rode to work together as a couple.

Then after the baby was born, it became a rarity to actually see us out somewhere together unless we had our son in tow. We had somehow forgotten how to be "MikeandJulie" and had in turn become "Ryan's Mommy and Daddy."

And perhaps you know where this is going: we began to drift apart from each other a little bit. We began to take one another for granted, each of us seeing the other as a coworker and taking the time to talk only when we had updates to deliver:

ME: Evenin', Julie.

JULIE: Howdy. How was your day?

ME: Exhausting! The boss was bustin' my hump.

JULIE: Bad day, eh?

ME: He was all over me. "Wipe this" and "Wipe that" and "Elmo this" and "Elmo that."

JULIE: That sucks. I'm probably going to be on his shit list tonight because I didn't read "Mr. Brown Can Moo, Can You?" before bedtime last night.

ME: Yeah, he mentioned that you were going to get a written warning over that one. He was in a pretty foul mood. And it was worse first thing this morning. You know how he gets if he hasn't had his morning cup of juice.

JULIE: Any messages for me?

ME: Yeah. Hell called. They want their baby back.

JULIE: Well, there's the whistle. My shift is starting. Gotta go.

ME: Good luck to ya. I'm going to go drink until I'm blind. Good to see you.

JULIE: We should get together sometime.

ME: Yes, we should. How does the year 2018 look for you?

Luckily, Julie and I soon came to grips with this situation and began trying to think of solutions to the problem. We both realized that we were starting to fall into a rut, a rut so deep that the psycho from *Silence of the Lambs* could have fit his victims down in it.

As a way to deal with our problem, Julie and I had to make it a point to start having "date nights" with each other. These nights would range from hiring a babysitter to watch Ryan while we went to a movie or out to dinner or to even doing something as simple as having Ryan watch a video in his room while we just sat alone and talked (or if I got lucky, I'd . . . um . . . get lucky, if you get my drift). And suddenly we were back to being "Mike and Julie" or "MikeandJulie" instead of just "Ryan's parents," if only for a brief while. It was wonderful, and a great way for us to reconnect as a couple. And it is a very essential part of parenting.

So, listen to me, reader: if you take nothing else from this book, please remember this: It is incredibly important to retain your identity as a person and as a married couple once you also add "parents" to your identity. If you get too lost in your role as a parent, your other relationships begin to suffer. We see it all too often in other families (and sometimes in ours) where the priorities shift too far in the other direction and you begin to forget what made you a great family in the first place. It is also healthy for your toddler to go spend some time with a sitter. This way they know that you are not the only people in their world, and that when you go somewhere, you will come back. It's not like their parents are disappearing into thin air; they leave as well as come back. And maintaining a healthy, happy relationship with each other will show your child how to truly love.

So there is a way to maintain a good balance between your key roles as parents and as a couple: Every now and then, take your coworker out, leave your boss with a babysitter, and go have a much-needed after-work beer. But unlike at your normal workplace, you can pork your coworker without having HR breathing down your neck.

End of Chapter Review Questions

What have we learned here?

1. What exactly do babies dream about, anyway? Maybe they long for the days of going back up into the birth canal. God knows I think about that special area at least fifty times a day.

2. What is the best way to keep your marriage and love life relevant after becoming parents?

    a. Spending quality time alone as a couple.
    b. Joining a support group for parents with toddlers.
    c. Attending social functions for adults only while trying not to discuss the latest episode of *Spongebob Squarepants.*
    d. Having a three-way with the eighteen-year-old babysitter.

3. This isn't a question so much as a strongly worded suggestion: Make sure you run a background check on your babysitter to ensure that she is at least eighteen and of legal age. I'm just sayin'. . . .

11

···

From Parents
to Grandparents—
Darwin's Forgotten Evolution

···

FROM STEVE, A REAL *GUY'S GUIDE* GUY:

When I was a kid, my dad wouldn't let me get away with shit, dude. He would catch me at every little thing I tried to do. It was like he had eyes in the back of his head. If I were about to screw up, he somehow anticipated it and busted me immediately. If I even thought about doing something bad, he'd whip my butt. I'll never forget one time when I had stolen a beer from our garage and my friends and I went to the woods to split it between the four of us. When we got to the special "meeting" place in the woods, my dad was there waiting on us. To this day I don't know how he knew about it, but he somehow got there before us. And right there in front of my friends, he yanked the beer out of my hands, bent me over his knee, and whaled on me. My butt was red for a week.

Now that he is a grandparent, he lets my daughter get away with murder. If she throws a fit in the middle of a mall, he says shit like, "She's just tired" or "It's OK, Steve. She's acting like a toddler because she is a toddler, so give her a break." Never mind that if I had pulled that crap on him he would have wanted to kill me. I don't know what happened to the old dad that I used to have and how he became this other guy. But I sure would have liked to have been around that "other" guy the day I was caught with that beer.

I am not about to go into the old debate of "evolution vs. creationism," mainly because I'm not nearly smart enough to back up either argument with sound reasoning. I'm not going to preach to you. I'm not going to try to prove to you that there is or is not a God, that Darwin was right or wrong, that one religion is better or worse than another. Hell, I'm not even going to try to say whether or not the old phrase "beer before liquor, never sicker" is or is not a truism. But there is at least one part of evolution theory that I believe Charles Darwin gave short shrift and that is worth discussing here.

Too interested in animals, Darwin missed the freaky evolution happening in real time. Indeed, if he could explain to me how my parents evolved from "tyrants with Nazi-like punishment policies" to "sweet and loving grandparents who would let the grandson get away with anything short of an Enron-esque scandal," I would gladly be driving around with one of those stickers on the back of my car that has a fish with feet saying "Darwin" on it.

Old Chuck D.—as he liked to be called—really missed the boat on this one. If he could have explained how such an evolution occurred not only to my parents, but also to all parents, he would be much more respected in the Christian community. And had he done this, people around the globe would be celebrating his birthday the same way we now celebrate Christmas, Columbus Day, or President's Day: by having huge sales on mattresses and Hondas.

When I was a boy, I wasn't allowed to get away with anything. My parents were very straitlaced, conservative people. I was the typical only child of a pretty typical middle-class family. We lived at the end of a typical cul-de-sac deep in the heart of Middle America and led sort of a

Beaver Cleaver–type life. My parents were very attentive to my needs but at the same time they also didn't let me run all over them, either. I wouldn't describe their parental style as overly strict by any means, but they still didn't take any crap from me. I was punished when I did wrong, as I should have been.

But when my grandparents were around, their opinion was that my parents were being too hard on me. To my grandparents, it wouldn't have mattered if I'd have set fire to a church while stealing the parishioners' wallets. My grandparents would have figured out some logical and reasonable excuse for what I was doing. My grandmother frequently explained "He's just tired." Or she would claim that I "must not be feeling well." My mom, knowing me as well as she did, wouldn't buy it. She knew that I wasn't tired or feeling sick; I was being a dick. But in the eyes of my grandparents, I was golden. I was like a made man in the Mafia—untouchable. And as a result, I always thought my grandparents were the nicest people on the planet. They loved me no matter what, and defended me when my mean old parents were punishing me for such foolish little things as tantrums or throwing rocks at smaller children.

Of course, a miraculous transformation occurred once my parents became grandparents. Like their parents before them, they suddenly became all gooey-eyed at the very sight of their grandchild. He could do no wrong, and if I claimed otherwise I was suddenly the bad guy. There have been times when he has been acting up and I've turned to my mother with an eye roll and a this-kid-is-driving-me-bananas look on my face. And what did my mom say to me? "Oh, he's just tired." This woman, the same woman who thirty years earlier wanted to throw punches at her mother-in-law for saying something moronic like "he's just tired" was now using that bullshit line on me.

I pointed this out to her. My mom explained her reasoning to me. It seemed that since she didn't see him every waking second of every day like I did, Ryan's escapades and fits were "cute" to her. To give you an example, here is a typical phone conversation between my parents and me:

ME: Hi, Mom.

MOM: Hey! Whatcha doin'?

ME: Watching Spongebob for the forty-second consecutive time today. What are you guys . . .

MOM: I think your dad's on the phone. Ron, are you there?

(I hear rustling in the background and my father mumbles something about what a piece of crap their old phone is.)

MOM: Ron, are you there?

DAD: Quit yelling into the phone! I'm sitting right next to you!

MOM: Well, you weren't saying anything. I wasn't sure you can hear me.

ME: Don't let me interrupt you folks. This is only costing me precious cell phone minutes.

DAD: Well, you know how she is.

MOM: Hey!

DAD: Turn the TV down, I can't hear Mike.

MOM: WHAT? I CAN'T HEAR YOU! THE TV'S TOO LOUD!

DAD: Don't yell into the phone! I'm right here!

(Sound of me spinning the chamber of a pistol in preparation of the ensuing game of Russian roulette.)

MOM: So, how's the boy?

ME: He's fine, I guess. He's been grumpy today. He won't leave me alone, and I really need to get stuff done. I've got a deadline and I can't get any work done with him hanging on me all day.

MOM: Oh, he's just tired.

DAD: Maybe he doesn't feel good.

ME: No, he's fine. He's just being ugly today. He's a toddler. It happens.

MOM: There is nothing wrong with that boy! Are you being mean to him?

ME: Mean? No, I'm not being mean! I . . .

MOM: You be nice to that sweet little boy!

DAD: Stop yelling into the phone, woman!

MOM: Shut up!

ME: OK, that's enough. I gotta go.

MOM: Why?

ME: I don't know. I don't feel good. I'm tired.

MOM: You're fine. You're just being grumpy!

ME: How is it that when Ryan's being a jerk, he's just tired. But when I'm not feeling well, I'm being a jerk?

MOM: You just be nice to that sweet little grandbaby. Give him a kiss for me!

DAD: I can't hear anything. This phone's a piece of crap.

MOM: I told him to kiss Ryan for us and. . . .

DAD: Stop yelling into the phone!

ME: I gotta go. The house ran away and the cat is on fire. Bye.

DAD: What?

MOM: Bye!

DAD: Stop yelling!

It dawns on me at this critical juncture in my psychological development (or at this point in the manuscript, anyway) that while most difficult or uncomfortable moments in parenting stem from separation anxiety (ours *and* our kids'), grandparents go through a certain amount of separation anxiety also. I actually realized it once talking to my parents about this subject as I was preparing to write about it. They explained to me that the feeling of painful separation is magnified by the miles that separate us now. They feel as though they're missing out on their only grandson's childhood. As a result, they want the time they do get to spend with him to be happy, and so they convince themselves that this child is golden and without sin. And in knowing that they feel this way, I always feel that it's my duty to make sure Ryan is in top form when they're around.

When he was two and three years old, I never wanted them to see him act like a typical toddler; I wanted them to think he was always an angelic and special child. So when he did start to act like the two-year-old that he was, I wanted to nip that behavior in the bud immediately. Little did I realize that he could shoot the Pope and somehow they'd think it was cute. "Oh, doesn't he have just the best aim for someone his age? Such hand/eye coordination on this one! Sure, he assassinated a religious figure, but he must be tired. Or maybe he's teething and doesn't feel well."

Darwin really needed to spend less time on monkeys and more time on grandparents. That's all I'm sayin'. (But now that I think about it, monkeys and grandparents aren't all that dissimilar. Both groups wear diapers, eat mushy things like bananas, and walk a little hunched over. . . .)

End of Chapter Review Questions

What have we learned here?

1. What is the main cause for grandparents to react sweeter to their grandchildren than they did to us when we were kids?

    a. They felt it was their duty as parents to be strict and stern with us as children, teaching us right from wrong.

    b. Senility.

    c. They like the grandkids more than us.

2. Seriously, why do people of a certain age refuse to throw away the old phones that have permanently tangled cords and make more crackling noises than a ham radio?

3. When did Darwin first pen his theory of natural selection?

    a. 1836

    b. 1835

    c. Shortly after realizing that there are actually fans of the movie *Ernest Goes to Jail.*

12

Screwing the Stork—
Explaining Sex to a Toddler

FROM FRANKLIN, A REAL *GUY'S GUIDE* GUY:

I'll never forget the moment I realized that being a dad of two boys meant that at some point I would have to answer uncomfortable sex questions. I was sitting at the breakfast table, drinking coffee, when I noticed my four-year-old son Dougie squirming in his seat across from me. After watching him wiggle around for a few minutes, my curiosity got the best of me and I asked him what was bothering him. Never did I expect what came out of his mouth. "Dad, I feel like I need to pee, but I can't because my wiener is too hard and it won't go down." After, spraying hot coffee all over the morning edition, I shrugged him off and told him to go try to pee one more time. Problem solved and an uncomfortable answer avoided or so I thought. A few minutes later when he returned from the bathroom to inform me that he still couldn't go and that his wiener was still hard, I realized that I would have to go where no father wants to go. Just as I braced myself to explain to him the anatomy of the human male and hormones, his younger brother, Houston, came to my rescue. "I know what to do," he said. "When my wiener gets hard, I just smack it and rub it and play with it a lot and eventually it goes back down to normal!" Thank God for younger brothers. Who would've thought that my two-year-old would be the one to teach my oldest about masturbation? I just hope he knows about other facets, too, because I'm not sure I'm cut out for this part of parenting. If not, I guess I could always write books like you do.

One day a little boy says to his parents, "Mommy, where do babies come from?" to which the mother replies, "From the stork, of course." And her little boy looks at her with a confused expression on his face and says, "Yeah, but who fucks the stork?" I think that joke is hilarious, although I must apologize to the author of the joke, as I don't know who originated it and cannot give them their due credit.

Explaining sex to a child of any age, let alone a toddler, is a daunting task. I dreaded the conversation, but as the father of a toddler, I was heartened to know that it would be many years before I had to broach it. This was one stage I didn't want to have Ryan get to quickly. But as with all things that I firmly believe won't happen to me when they happen to me, the sex talk reared its ugly head not long after Ryan turned three. You heard me, three. Pretty early.

And as with most important moments of parenthood, I found that I was not remotely prepared for this talk. And for that I blame my parents.

My parents—an electrician and a housewife—have a rather conservative sense of humor, and so as I was growing up we didn't joke about sex. We didn't talk about sex. We didn't watch TV shows or movies that involved sex. (In fact, the raciest thing I was allowed to watch back then was "Bugs Bunny," and even his motives were in question whenever he wore a dress to fool Elmer Fudd.) And as far as I'm concerned my parents never even had sex. I've long believed that my birth was an immaculate conception, second in the history of Man only to Jesus' birth to Mary and Joseph. I was born to a virgin. (And for my own sanity, I need to believe in my heart of hearts that this is true.)

There were only two times in my childhood when I can remember bringing up the subject of sex. And both times ended up with me knowing just as little as before I asked. The first time I inquired about sex (and in this case I wasn't asking about porking so much as I was asking about gender) was when I was about three years old. I had walked into the bedroom and saw my mother changing her clothes. I asked her at that point why she didn't look the same as I did and why she had hair "down there." My mother looked me straight in the eye and asked me a very important question: "Do you want a lollipop?" Of course I said, "Sure!" and then I went about my day and totally forgot about my question.

The second time I inquired about sex came a few years later. I overheard my mom telling one of her friends that my dad had gotten a vasectomy. Not knowing what one was, I asked my dad to explain. "Dad," I said sweetly. "What's a vasectomy?"

He stammered for a moment and finally said, "Uh . . . I don't know." He promptly left the room.

Between the lollipops and the "I don't knows," I'm glad I didn't ask any more questions, or I'd have ended up diabetic and stupid at the same time. As it stands now, I'm just stupid. And that's just fine by me.

I don't think I learned a thing about sex—the act (I did fundamentally understand that there are two genders, even if I didn't yet understand how they worked together to make babies)—until I was nearing double-digits. I learned about it the way a lot of Generation X kids first discovered the truth about sex: HBO. I can remember sneaking out into the living room and watching cable television while my parents slept. I would tiptoe through the house and creep ever-so-quietly into the living room, turn on the television with the volume down so low that I could barely even hear it and see all the "dirty" things that Hollywood had to offer. I can remember watching old comedy concerts by Richard Pryor and Eddie Murphy, and laughing my ass off at jokes that—while I didn't understand them fully—were filled with naughty words that I would soon be teaching to friends on the street. Who'd have thought that one insulated wire running directly into the back of an old Zenith TV, would not only entertain, but educate me as well?

During one of my late-night "sneak peeks," I happened to stumble across a movie called *Body Heat*, a rather steamy and sexual version of *Double Indemnity* starring Kathleen Turner. Perhaps you've seen it? Several times? During one sex scene, it suddenly dawned on me what this whole sex thing was about. I can remember thinking to myself, *I have to . . . put my . . . up and . . . inside of her . . . oh God! That sounds disgusting! Wait a minute . . . that's where she pees! GROSS! I never want to do that!*

I have since changed my stance on the subject, by the way. Oh boy, have I ever. . . . But that's another book. Actually, it's already on the market: *The Guy's Guide to Dating, Getting Hitched, and Surviving the First Year of Marriage,* by yours truly. Perhaps you've read it? Hey, every book needs a shameless plug for another. It's called product placement these days. But I digress. (My God, I'm such a whore. . . .)

So, we've established here that my parents gave me no sex education. Given this, I had decided early on that I would not be so cheap with the info with my son. I was going to be completely honest and forthcoming with him when he brought up the subject. Sex is, after all, an integral part of how we all came to be, and learning about it is an integral element of growing up. Ryan deserved no less than the truth. I would not pull that stork crap on my only child. I wouldn't tell him that "Angels floated down on clouds and gently laid babies down on the doorstops of the new parents" or any of that shit. I was going to be open and honest, and would do anything just shy of giving him a live demonstration to school him in the ways of procreation.

And I truly thought I would stick to that plan. I thought so right up until the moment he asked me the following dreaded question:

"Daddy, where do babies come from? And how did I get out of mommy's belly?"

First of all, I didn't think he would ask so soon. He was only three at the time. Young right? So the fact that his little inquisitive mind wanted to understand the beginnings of life so early caught me off guard. (And oddly enough, I had just had a vasectomy of my very own!)

This was the moment of truth: would I fill my son's little mind with bullshit, give him the God's honest truth, or present him with a hybrid of the two? Just before I started painting verbal images of a gigantic bird carrying a newborn in a picnic basket to the local hospital, it dawned on me that Ryan really just wanted to know the bare minimum. His questions were really about geography and transportation, not biology. He wasn't particularly interested in how he got *into* his mother's stomach. He just wanted to know how he got *out* of his mother's stomach. So Julie and I explained that mommies and daddies head off to the hospital, mommies push for a while, and babies eventually come out.

Thank God we had this conversation with him after he had already potty-trained, because he probably would have thought he himself was going into labor twice a day and would feel bad about dropping his baby into the toilet.

Ryan then asked if boys have babies, too. Ah, we could see where this was going. We explained that no, boys do not give birth to babies. We explained that it was the way God made women, and thanks to Eve committing the first sin, women now deserved all the pain they felt during labor. (Just kidding; wanted to see if you were paying attention.) We told him that women have the babies and he would never have to worry about giving birth (but notice we didn't say he'd never have to worry about having a baby—it's all in the spin, my friend).

Ryan sat silently for a while, thinking about what we had just told him. Eventually he perked up and said, "I'm glad I'm not a girl." And all I could think was, *Me too, son. Me, too.* Because in having a son, a father only has to worry about one boy. When you're the father of a daughter, you have to worry about a million boys.

But it occurred to me then that maybe, just maybe, the "sex talk" wouldn't be the worst subject I'd have to tackle. After all, talking about sex seems infinitely easier than trying to explain things like death, God, Satan, heaven, hell, terrorism, politics, and how Michael Jackson went from being a black man to a white woman. Hell, I can't even understand that last one. And try explaining Hitler to a tod-dler. See how well you fare, and then decide how much simpler it would be just telling them about how men and women get it on.

Still, I see now why my parents didn't want to have the sex talk too early (if at all). It's not that I don't think Ryan could have handled knowing the facts—all the facts. He's a bright kid and is always willing to learn something new. But there is a certain amount of inno-cence lost when you discover the truth about where life begins. And kids are already growing up too quickly these days. So who am I to derail his youthful look at the world with the facts of life? I'm sure in a few years he'll be quite interested about the ins and outs of sex, pardon the pun. And at that time, I'm sure I'll tell him more than he ever wanted to know, and he'll never be able to look at me or his mother the same way again. But for the time being, I think answering only his direct questions—offering information to address exactly what he is ask-ing—is the way to go. That let's me off the hook for a few more years, anyway.

And Dad, if you're reading this . . . it's time we had the talk. I'm thirty-six now, after all. And Julie would probably appreciate it if I actually knew what I was doing.

End of Chapter Review Questions

What have we learned here?

1. Isn't HBO a wonderful thing?
    a. Yes
    b. No
    c. I don't know. I'm too cheap to pay twelve dollars for the satellite company to allow me to have it.

2. When teaching a toddler about sex, what is the best way to describe the act?
    a. Be completely honest with the child.
    b. Show her books and diagrams.
    c. Tell her that you can get pregnant by kissing while wearing a bathing suit, and that she should never, ever do it.

3. Do you ever wonder who thought of a vasectomy in the first place? I'm guessing it was first performed on a stay-at-home dad, and he probably did the surgery himself after spending too much "quality time" with his children.

4. What exactly was Hitler's problem, anyway? Man, what a dick!

13

The Secret Society

FROM TED, A REAL *GUY'S GUIDE* GUY:

Getting my boys into preschool was no small feat. I have triplets, so finding room for all three of them was difficult enough in and of itself. I know it's hard to get one child to the top of a waiting list for a good school, let alone three. We asked around in our community to find out what the best school was for them to attend, and we made a list of five or so of the highest recommended schools. My wife began calling each school one-by-one to see if they had any openings for the following fall semester, and of course none of them had any openings. If they did, they certainly didn't have three. Just as we were about to give up on this quest, one of the schools called. They said that they had a couple of families move away unexpectedly, as a manufacturing plant in our town had gone under. Since these children had left the school, they now had three spots open for our boys. They set an appointment for us to come in and meet with the administrators. My wife and I figured that we would be touring the facility, meeting the teachers, and then writing a huge deposit check for all the first month of our sons' tuitions. But when we got there, it became more of an interview than an orientation. My sons had to answer questions to test their intelligence. Their behavior was being scrutinized, as were our views on parenting and religion. We must not have overly impressed the staff, because our sons were rejected from that preschool. We said screw it and ended up keeping our kids at home. To this day, they are home schooled and will probably never see the inside of one of those places. I think we're better off.

I've already told you that I stayed at home with Ryan the first few years of his life, so it shouldn't come as a surprise to you that preparing to send him to preschool presented me with an emotional dilemma. I had spent every waking hour since the beginning of 2000 caring for Ryan, tending to his every want and need. It was a conscious decision on my part and of Julie's to have a parent stay home with Ryan. And I was the one tapped with this duty. Let's face it, I don't need to go to an office, clock in, sit at a desk drinking coffee from a mug that says, "I Have a Case of the Mondays" and flirt with a voluptuous, buxom secretary in order to write these books that mainly consist of booger and baby-shit jokes. In fact, truth be told, the most taxing part of my day usually involves trying to decide what adjective best describes the color of newborn baby poop in a funny enough manner to warrant putting into these *Guy's Guides*.

Once Ryan was old enough to start interacting with other children, however, it became increasingly clear that he might lack the social proficiency he'd need by the time kindergarten rolled around. Case in point: at the local playground the kids in Monday through Friday day care tended to be playful with each other; Ryan was happiest singing an AC/DC song to a stick over by the swing set, some hundred yards away from the others. We've missed a lot of cues in our time, but this hint we took: Ryan needed some playmates his own age, and a little less quality time with his rock 'n' roll–obsessed father. Couple that with the fact that I was going out of my goddamn mind having to chase this child around all day, and you will see why Julie and I decided that now was the time to look into preschool (for Ryan, not me).

Upon hearing of his acceptance to a local country club, Groucho Marx once said "I would never join a club that would have me as a member." I love this quote but Groucho obviously never had problems getting his son, Arthur, or daughters Miriam and Melinda into a preschool in the twenty-first century. The series of hoops that a family has to jump through in order to enroll a child into a good preschool is so ridiculous that it would almost be humorous, if you weren't spending time, energy, and money in the process. It's a nerve-wracking experience, and I for one am glad Mr. Marx never had to endure the enrollment process in a modern-day preschool. (Besides, Groucho's son, Arthur, is in his mid-eighties now and probably wouldn't get along with the children anyway.)

But I've jumped ahead of my story. Initially, Julie and I thought that gaining Ryan entrée to a good preschool would be a piece of cake. How hard could it really be, right? We weren't living in New York City, where preschool enrollment is legendarily hard. No, we simply wanted Ryan to have a few hours a day with his peers, and we knew there were lots of places where that could be arranged.

Alas, nearly every reputable school in a fifty-mile radius was filled up. Furthermore, every single one of them seemed to be overflowing with kids. Each place was lousy with them. In most cases, it was one kid after another, lined up asshole to belly button. The waiting lists were lengthy for the really good schools; some waiting lists had waiting lists. Still, we persevered. If Ryan was ever going to have a shot at getting to socialize with his peers, we'd need to place his name on a list.

But even getting your child's name on a waiting list turns out to be close to impossible. I wanted to shout: "I have money for you. Take it, find this child a tiny little chair to sit his tiny little ass in and let me get on with my tiny little life, for the love of God! I have books filled with tiny little jokes to write. I don't have time for this shit!"

But the old law of supply and demand takes precedent in the world of preschools. The schools were getting their money already from the folks who were smart enough to get their kid on the waiting list six months before they were even born. But since they had what we wanted (and not the other way around), the schools could be picky as to who they allowed to grace their classrooms. It seemed that getting Ryan into a preschool that would have him was becoming a task greater and more difficult than cracking *The Da Vinci Code*, although it was infinitely more entertaining. (But bear in mind, that's coming from an author who's jealous that my books don't sell 100 million copies and become movies starring Tom Hanks, so feel free to dismiss that last joke.)

Indeed, each school called us in for a preliminary screening and interview process before we could get Ryan on the waiting list for the waiting list. They wanted to assess Ryan's overall preschool readiness—both academic and behavioral. Each interviewer asked him his name, asked him to identify letters of the alphabet, and strove to find out how high he could count. Going in I thought we had it made each time—I was confident that he knew his own name and that he could be able to sing his ABCs and 123s. But again—and you could have seen this coming—I was to be wrong yet again.

Subjects that he knew like the back of his hand, such as counting or going through the alphabet would somehow escape him once he was asked about them by the administrator who was interviewing us. And in contrast, he somehow had a grasp on other things that I had no idea he was aware of. With every passing interview, I became more perplexed, and tried to help my little guy focus on the task at hand. An average interview went something like this:

SCHOOL ADMINISTRATOR: Hi there. What's your name?

ME: His name is Ryan.

SCHOOL ADMINISTRATOR: Please, Mr. Crider. Let him answer for himself.

ME: Sorry. Go on. Tell the nice lady your name.

RYAN: Ryan.

SCHOOL ADMINISTRATOR: OK, Ryan. I'm going to give you a little test here just to see what a big boy you are. Are you ready?

RYAN: I like French fries.

ME: No, no. She said . . .

SCHOOL ADMINISTRATOR: Please, Mr. Crider.

ME: Sorry.

SCHOOL ADMINISTRATOR: Um . . . OK. First of all, can you count to ten for me?

RYAN: Sure! 1,2,3, potato, 7.

ME: What? You know how to count to ten! What are you doing?

SCHOOL ADMINISTRATOR: Mr. Crider . . .

ME: Sorry.

SCHOOL ADMINISTRATOR: OK, Ryan. Do you know your ABCs?

RYAN: Yeah!

SCHOOL ADMINISTRATOR: Very good. Do you know how old you are?

RYAN: I don't know.

ME: What do you mean you don't know? What the fu . . .

SCHOOL ADMINISTRATOR: *Mr. Crider! There are children present!*

ME: Sorry.

SCHOOL ADMINISTRATOR: OK, Ryan. Can you tell me the molecular formula of a hydrocarbon?

RYAN: Um . . . is it C_nH_m?

SCHOOL ADMINISTRATOR: Yes, very good!

ME: You don't know how old you are or how to count to ten, but you've somehow managed to master quantum physics?

SCHOOL ADMINISTRATOR: (glaring at me)

ME: Sorry.

After this kind of embarrassing exchange, we were always told that we would be put on the waiting list for the waiting list. Or if I were really neurotic during the interview process, he would be put on the waiting list for the waiting list's waiting list. This was usually followed by a long, silent trip home with my wife staring at me like I was a complete dumbass. That is when I knew that I had screwed the pooch, and we moved onto the next school and the next embarrassing failure.

It was clear to me then, and it is even more clear to me now: none of this was a failure on Ryan's part. He did the best he could, and in his defense, the mind of a three-year-old boy is usually too busy thinking about toys, scary bugs that want to eat you, and whatever animated program he last saw on Nickelodeon. So I don't blame him for the failed interviews. It was really my own neuroses that got us into these situations repeatedly. I think I not only wanted him to be accepted into the school and for him to impress the administrator, I also wanted to show the school that I was doing my job as a parent. Whenever he didn't know something easy like his ABCs or his numbers, I felt like I was being judged as a slacker parent. It was a matter of pride.

There's a happy ending to this little story, of course: we finally found a school that was somehow able to overlook Ryan's idiot father, and he was accepted into his very first classroom experience. My checking account was finally liberated of its contents. And before I knew it, I had gotten my wish. Ryan would soon be out of the house and I would get my life back. Little did I know that I would immediately be missing him the second he walked out the door.

End of Chapter Review Questions

What have we learned here?

1. What should your child know before entering pre-school?
   a. The three R's
   b. The Three Stooges
   c. The three singers of Van Halen

2. What is a good and funny way to describe the color of poop found in an infant's diaper?
   a. Honey mustard
   b. Pup-tent green
   c. Nuclear

3. A question for Dan Brown, the author of *The Da Vinci Code*: Can I borrow some money?

14

Sending Him Off to War

FROM CARL, A REAL *GUY'S GUIDE* GUY:

I'm probably going to get my balls taken away by my guy friends for saying this, but I cried like a baby the day my daughter went off to school for the first time. It was as if she was going away to college or something, even though I knew that she would be home in a few hours. She was so brave, dressed up in her pink dress that she called her "Cinderella Dress" with that bow in her hair and her ballet shoes. The whole way to school I kept telling her how she was going to make new friends. I told her I didn't want her to be nervous, and that she would do great. But she didn't really seem nervous at all. I think I was trying to ease my own fears. Once we got to school, I kissed her, gave her a big hug, and then watched as she walked to her classroom. Just as she got to her door, she turned around and waved at me with a tear in her eye. Then she started running back toward me while screaming at the top of her lungs, "I don't wanna do this!" By the time she reached me, she was crying her eyes out. I told her that she had to go and that she'd do great. So I walked her into her classroom, where she immediately saw a Barbie doll and started playing with it. She forgot about being sad and forgot that I was even there. I called the school every hour or so to check on her, and every time the teacher said she was doing fine. And in the end, she did do fine. I cried the rest of the day.

As I said at the very beginning of this book, from the minute I cut the cord and freed Ryan from his mother's womb, there are a few things I started looking forward to. I looked forward to the time a couple of days later when I would be getting my baby boy home to begin our lives as father and son. Then as soon as he got home and started crying his little lungs out, I looked forward to him going away to college so I could have my sanity back. Don't get me wrong, I loved my infant son, and I love being his daddy. I think it's more fair to say that I wanted Ryan to get a little older so he could be a real person instead of the screeching thing that sent our cat running for cover under the bed for the better part of a year.

But as I've said before, be careful what you wish for— you might just actually get it. Because in what seemed like the blink of an eye, my infant was now a little boy: A walking, talking, potty-pooper of a little boy who was now getting ready to go to preschool. As much as I had previously reveled in the thought of getting Ryan off to school and out of the house for a while, some strange feeling came over me when it came time to actually do it. As a parent—particularly a stay-at-home parent—you begin to think that you're the only person who could possibly handle your child's specific needs. Even though deep down you realize that the teachers in these schools are better trained to deal with children than even most parents are, it is still an uneasy feeling to just say, "Here's the person I created and have seen every waking minute since he spilled out of my wife's uterus. Mold him into a learning machine." Call it paranoia. Call it separation anxiety. Call it what you will. But as much as I wanted Ryan to become more grown-up, the very thought made me so nervous that I thought I'd certainly die of ulcers or a stroke before the time came for me to pick him up at the end of the day.

That first morning started out much differently than any other day of Ryan's life. For starters, we had to wake him up as opposed to him waking us up (as had been the tradition since his very first day home from the hospital). Julie and I both went in to wake him up, and he looked at us like, "What the hell are you doing waking me up this early in the morning?" Once we finally wrangled him out of the bed, we got him dressed, had breakfast, and got ready for his big day. We took pictures of him in front of a tree outside to commemorate our big boy's first day of school, packed his little lunch box and soon I sent him off on his way. As he was leaving in the car with his mother, Ryan waved at me and with a teary eye he said, "I'm really gonna miss you, Daddy." At this point, the part of me that had been thrilled at the thought of regaining my freedom for a few childless hours had disappeared. I was now left with an aching feeling in my chest, an empty nest, and the overwhelming feeling that I was wrong to want my son to grow up so soon.

The cliché is that "you don't know what you've got until it's gone." And that saying really rang true for me when Ryan started school. Of course, there's also a saying that goes, "Shit rolls downhill," but that's a completely different story.

I had an instant feeling of emptiness as soon as Ryan went off to his first day at school. The very thing I had been hoping for finally came about, and suddenly I missed the little fella so badly that it hurt. I missed the questions: "Why? Why? Why?" I wanted my boy to come home. As it turns out, that first day was no picnic for him, either.

When I went to pick Ryan up from his first day at pre-school (a whopping five hours away from me in one sitting), I noticed for the first time (or I was encouraged to notice) that the walls of his classroom were painted with bright primary colors and were covered with kids' artwork. There were posters on the wall that showed every letter in the alphabet as well as pictures of items that started with each letter. With the exception of the mud stains from the children's shoes, years of smashed crayons that had been ground down into the fibers, and, of course, vomited peanut-butter-and-jelly sandwiches from students past, the room was mostly rainbow colored. All in all not a bad place to be, I thought.

I looked around for Ryan, expecting him to be playing with the other kids. The girls were playing with dolls and having tea parties for their Barbie dolls. The boys were roughhousing, or playing with cars and trucks, using them to crash into the girls' tea parties and doing their best to behead all of the Barbie dolls. But as I looked around, I didn't see my son anywhere. Then I looked at the teacher's desk and my heart sank.

Ryan was sitting on his teacher's lap. And apparently that's where he had spent a majority of his day. Being that he didn't normally spend time with kids his age, Ryan hadn't known how to interact with the class. He clearly felt more comfortable talking to the teachers and other adults at the school. When he saw that I was there to pick him up and "rescue" him, his little eyes lit up like a Christmas tree, or to be more specific, his eyes lit up like a Christmas tree whose daddy came to pick it up from a long day at Christmas tree school. (I have absolutely no idea what that means, by the way. But it's a hell of a visual, don't you think?) He had a folder to show me, filled with the work he had done for the day. There were paintings, drawings, and little balls of mutilated clay that were supposed to pass as art. The ashtray he had made for me and his mother more resembled a dried pile of cow crap. But then I suppose art, by its very nature, is subjective.

Ryan waved good-bye to his teacher with one hand while grabbing onto me with his other hand in a death grip that I suppose was his way of saying, "Don't you ever leave me alone again." When we got out to my car, I asked him how his day was. He told me that it was fun. I asked him what his favorite part was, and he said it was when they got to eat lunch in the school cafeteria. He just thought that was the coolest thing ever. Then he told me that he really liked his teacher, but he was glad it was all over with.

It took me a moment to realize it, but suddenly it dawned on me that he thought that this school thing was just a one-time deal. I realized that it was up to me to be the bearer of bad news. I explained to him that school would be a daily ritual for him, and that his schooling wouldn't technically be over with until at least high school. And not only that, but if he wanted to get a really good career he would have to attend at least four years of college. Or he could do like his daddy did; drink himself out of two colleges and just make money writing books about his own kid.

Ryan cried. A lot.

He cried, though I'm not sure if the tears were because he realized that he'd have about nineteen more years of schooling or if the thought of ending up like his father scared him completely shitless. Either way, he was not happy to hear that he would be spending the majority of his childhood in a classroom with other children. Knowing him, he'd have gladly spent the rest of his days watching *Thomas the Tank Engine* and sucking on juice pouches.

In the end, he eventually became used to the idea of school and I adjusted to the idea of not having him around the house every minute of the day. He had his good days and bad days at school, of course. On the good days, I felt happy that he was adjusting to his new schedule. But then other days he would rip my heart out by crying and telling me that he would miss me when he headed off with Julie to school. I too had my good days and bad days. On the good days, I knew in my heart that I was doing the right thing by helping him move on to this new stage in his life. I knew that he had to learn to deal with his peers and to get used to the learning environment because he would be faced with many years of school in the future. So on those days, I felt good about myself.

And on the bad days, I simply doubled my dose of Prozac to deal with the guilt I felt over shipping my only son off to the real and ugly and greedy and dangerous real world.

End of chapter review questions

What have we learned here?

1. How do children know just the right way to tug at a father's heart and reduce us to tears?
    a. Instinct.
    b. Too many movies on the Lifetime Movie Network.

    c. They learned it by spending time with their mother and she taught them the fine art of guilt trips.

2. How many clay ashtrays can one preschool-age child make during her art class in any single given school year?

    a. 5

    b. 10

    c. Enough to hold all of Keith Richards's cigarette butts for a twenty-four-hour period.

15

Let It Be

FROM JULIUS, A REAL *GUY'S GUIDE* GUY:

Had I known that I was going to grow so attached to my child before he was born, I don't know that I'd have had the guts to go through with this whole fathering thing. I didn't know that I could ever love something or someone so much and with all of my heart and soul. I didn't know I had the capacity to love and adore someone even more than I loved myself. I've heard of love at first sight, but never believed in it. The moment I first saw my kid, I knew I was a goner. And over time I sort of forgot what it was like to have a life before him. He is the apple of my eye, that boy. We do everything together. We play with his toys, play baseball, we go out to lunch together on my

*days off of work, and we are really close to one an-
other. I'm so attached to him that I don't want him to
grow up and move out. He is the best thing that ever
happened to me. I almost feel guilty for ever trying to
talk his mother into aborting him. Live and learn.*

Parenting is like nothing else in the world. The good
times are better than any high I'd ever experienced before.
Conversely, the bad times are soooooo bad that I'd rather
take a prison-type beating than deal with them. And I
know I'm not alone on this. I know that parents have been
feeling similar emotions for countless generations. But for
some reason we—as humans—continue this dance. We
keep repeating what our ancestors did and what their ancestors did before them. We keep having children. We keep
making the same mistakes we said we would never make,
we do the things our parents did that we swore we'd never
do, and we keep on doing these things without the sure
knowledge that the time and money we put into these children will pay off in the end. We keep taking that risk.

I know that I, too, will experience a moment when my
son grows up, looks me in the eye, and says those magical
words: "Dad, I flunked out of another school. But it's OK,
'cause I'm going to be in a rock band and make millions."
And my father will be standing right behind him, grinning

from ear to ear and laughing his ass off, because he'll know it was my turn to get the ungrateful treatment that I gave to him and that he gave to his father before him. The cycle continues, eh?

Since coming home from the maternity ward, Ryan has pissed on me, thrown up on me, kept me up all night while crying at the top of his lungs, eaten all of my food, bitched and moaned when he didn't get his way, taken over my television and VCR while forcing me to watch the same episodes of *Blue's Clues* over and over, cost me a small fortune in clothes and other child-rearing items. . . . I swear to God, if this were a marriage, I'd have wanted to leave it a long time ago. I never would put up with this kind of bullshit from any woman. And I know Julie feels the same way—she'd never take such treatment from any man.

But with a kid, with our kid, somehow it was all different. Maybe it was because I knew that he was my son and I—as his father—had a responsibility to him and to care for his every need. Or maybe I'm just half nuts and a glutton for punishment. Either way, the father/son relationship is different than any other relationship I've ever encountered. No matter how angry or crazy he ever made me, particularly during the terrible twos and threes, I always kissed him and told him I loved him at the end of the day. And when there were times that I wanted to get away for a "guy's night" because I just couldn't take anymore bonding time with my son, what happened? I ended up coming home early to tuck him in because I missed him so badly while I was gone and couldn't bear the thought of him going to sleep without me there to wish him sweet dreams and kiss his sweet little face.

In Ryan's early life, I spent a great deal of time looking forward to whatever was coming next. In fact, as I've said, I think I spent way too much time wanting to hurry things along. I wasn't terribly interested in what was happening at the time. I was busy looking at other families with older children and thinking, "Man I can't wait until Ryan can do that." I didn't "stop to smell the roses," as it were. But to be fair, there were more dirty diapers in our house than there were roses. The point is I never really paused to just enjoy the moment and truly appreciate what was going on at that time. Don't get me wrong; I gave that child more attention than most generations of fathers before me have bestowed on their children (or do we all feel that way?). He never really was left wanting for anything, be it attention, nourishment, or toys. But I don't think I ever truly just let him be a baby. I always wanted him to get older and bigger so we could do fun things together. I didn't anticipate that he would one day be seven years old and upstairs listening to Foo Fighters while playing video games and totally ignoring his old man (which is exactly what he is doing as of this writing). I never realized there would come a time where he didn't really "need" me anymore.

When that time came—quicker than I could have ever imagined—it hit me like a ton of bricks. And I know that technically he still needs me to care for him. After all, he can't drive himself to McDonald's yet. But it's not the same as it was in the beginning. That's not always a bad thing. But it's not always good, either.

And unless you weren't paying attention before, you know that I used to sing Ryan a tune from John Lennon's *Double Fantasy* the last record before he was murdered in 1980—and the song is called "Beautiful Boy." One line from the song says, "I can hardly wait to see you come of age, but I guess we'll both just have to be patient."

Well said, John.

(Of course, that's the same guy who said "I am the Walrus. Coo coo ca choo." So maybe I shouldn't put too much stock in what he had to say. It's still a catchy tune though, don't you think?)

In trying to wrap up this book, I asked my son a question. I wanted to know when he thought he would be old enough to move out of his mother and father's house and live on his own. He looked at me for a minute, thought carefully about his answer and said, "I think I'll be forty-seven."

So I guess I have a while before I have to worry about dealing with an empty nest.

I wonder if he and his wife will both be sleeping with Julie while I'm still stuck on the couch?

End of Book Review Questions

What have we learned here?

Are you sure you want to deal with raising a toddler? Wouldn't it be easier to just get a puppy instead?

ACKNOWLEDGMENTS

A FEW YEARS AGO I sat down and began writing a chronological account of my first year as a father. I didn't set out to write a book initially; it was just going to be a journal so that when my son became an adult he could read the way I was feeling during his mother's pregnancy and his first few months on the planet. My thought was that he would be able to read it and truly understand the highs and lows of my experience, and this would help him realize why his father—who at that point will no doubt be spending his declining years sitting in a wheelchair, babbling incoherently while reminiscing romantically about the Reagan era, and eating a disgusting mixture of whipped white beans and liquefied cornbread through a straw—was the kind of father he was. But as I continued writing down my memories, I realized that, "Hey, this might work as a parenting book." I casually mentioned it to my friend and mentor Arthur Marx, who then introduced me to the man who would soon become my agent, Frank Weimann. And out of that, a writing career was born. Little did I know that the goofy little booger and dick jokes I was toying around with were going to someday become *The Guy's Guide to Surviving Pregnancy, Childbirth, and the First Year of Fatherhood* and would start a series of family-related humor books including *The Guy's Guide to Dating, Getting Hitched, and Surviving the First Year of Marriage* and the title you hold in your hand at the moment. It's been an amazing, fun ride and I can't wait to see what happens next. There is so much that I am thankful for, and I want to take a minute to acknowledge those who helped me recognize my dream.

To be honest, I never thought an editor would "get" my humor. Writers often see their editors as the enemy; someone who takes the heart and soul out of their book and turns it into a glossy pile of commercial-friendly dog shit. So I was just sure that no editor would want to touch my humor with a ten-foot pole, and I was even more afraid of what they would do with it if they ever did decide to take a chance on my book. And then I came across Marnie

Cochran. She not only got what I was trying to do, but she encouraged me and guided me in the right direction to get my point across. Sure, she has to reel me in on occasion when I get too over the top, but she always has my best interest in mind, which is apparent at every step along the way. So Marnie, thank you again for believing in me and for all you do for your authors on a daily basis. However you define success, we've accomplished something extraordinary with those books. So thank you for everything.

I'd also like to say hello and thank you to my agent Frank Weimann at The Literary Group in New York, who takes thirty minutes out of each year to actually speak to me on the phone and in return asks only for fifteen percent of my annual earnings. Man, I want your job. I'm in the wrong field. But at least we make the most of those minutes. You're the best agent a lowly author like me could ask for, and I thank you for still taking time to work with the smallest fish in your pond. I'll never forget the time when I called you after watching the movie *Misery*, in which the main character (a writer played by James Caan) goes missing in a snowstorm and his agent calls around trying to find out what happened to him. I asked you why you never look out for me like that. You said (and I still get teary-eyed when I think about it), "Because I hate you." And how can I not love you for such a sweet answer?

Now here comes the big list of my nearest and dearest: Julie, for doing me the small favor of redefining my universe over seventeen years ago; Ryan, for laughing at his Daddy's jokes and for giving me constant inspiration; Ron and Myrna Crider (aka "Granny and Pops"); Earl and Dianna Akard ("Grandma and Pappy"); Brian, Gloria, Lisha, and Jonathon Crider; Doug Barnette; Mick and Gloria Carson; Ben and Carrie Long; Jessica Carson; Arthur Marx and family (your padre and uncles most definitely included); Jenny McCarthy; Sid Caesar; Kate Kazeniac-Burke and everyone else at Da Capo; Newman Communications; Pam Anderson; Chelsea Handler; Rachael Ray; Lari White; Stefanie Wilder-Taylor; Darlene Thornburg and family; Joanna Cotten; Doug Campbell; Mick and Duane Funderburke; Richard and Terri Sparks; John, Sara and Dona-Marie Sparks; the Thomas boys; Tom Rainey and family; Barbie Butler; Dawn Hull; Lisa Distefano; Hayley Ross and everyone else at Alliance Agency; Tracy Richman; Allison Smith; Robert Trowbridge; Brandie Gallutia; Stacy Van Cour; Stephanie and Brian Vrshek; Lenny and Jamie Franklin; Jennifer and Doug Mendl; Colleen Curtis and everyone at Firepit Friday; Atomic Blonde; Stephanie Denny; Chad Warrix and family; D-Tox; Greg Pope and family; Deborah Honeycutt; Dennis Morgan; Prentice Morgan; Shelley Rogers and family; Laura Roudebush;

Emma Bowen Meyer; Hope Garner; Tiffany Tidwell-Atkins; Drew Herche; Nate Helyer; Kevin Vickery; Cory Stewart; Dave and Jennifer Easton; Rebecca Bullion and Dr. Michelle Cochran for showing me the light at the end of the tunnel (at a reasonable price); Warren Bullock and family; Sara Dishman; Kerry and Cindy Glisson; Ty Hunt; Holland Nix; Misty Garrity; 4/5 of The Dumpster Hogs; Lanore Haley and family; Nicole Gill; Misha Joseph; Gabby and Jim Lutton; Polly McCord (my teacher, mentor, and friend); Stacey Grosh; Tom Taylor; Sam Hill; Jeff Raymer; Megan Reveles; and whoever invented the "T9" function on my cell phone (it makes texting so much easier, doesn't it?).

MICHAEL CRIDER is the author of the highly acclaimed parenting book, *The Guy's Guide to Surviving Pregnancy, Childbirth, and the First Year of Fatherhood*, which received *Parent-to-Parent* magazine's Adding Wisdom Award for 2005. His follow-up effort, the humorous relationship guide entitled *The Guy's Guide to Dating, Getting Hitched, and Surviving the First Year of Marriage*, was released in early 2007. His fiction piece, *From Afar*, was released in

2003 and read by roughly six people (five of whom actually enjoyed it). He lives in Tennessee with his wife Julie and their son, Ryan. When he's not busy writing, he enjoys scuba diving, kayaking, and checking his books' daily sales ranks on Amazon.com.